IT'S BEYOND WORDS

IT'S THE ART OF CALCULATED COMMUNICATION

HAROLD WILKERSON

Copyright © 2025

All Rights Reserved.

Dedication

For Chayse Wilkerson.

Reaching your goals is not as far as you think. They are only as far as you can think.

For Shante Wilkerson—my driving force to run through walls.

Everyone wants to live forever, but the only way to achieve that is to make a difference or make history.

Acknowledgment

To my beloved family.

Susan Smith, without what you instilled in us, I would not be here. Thank you for making us wake up early to pack bags and deliver newspapers.

Harold Wilkerson Jr. (Jab), from Dad to mentor.

168 Nelson Avenue, Bronx, New York,

Noonan Plaza Apt BD.

Thank you.

Contents

Dedication i

Acknowledgment ii

About the Author iv

Preface vi

Introduction viii

Chapter 1: Intrapersonal Intelligence 1

Chapter 2: Interpersonal Communication 17

Chapter 3: Intercultural Communication 54

Chapter 4: Media & Manipulation 66

Chapter 5: Emotional Intelligence 91

Chapter 6: Leadership and Communication 101

Chapter 7: Power and Communication 107

Chapter 8: Persuasion and Communication 116

Chapter 9: Seductive Communication 123

Reviews on RateMyProfessor 124

References 126

About the Author

Harold Wilkerson is a multifaceted entertainment industry leader and visionary entrepreneur. Hailing from the Highbridge section of the Bronx, New York, Harold's remarkable journey is a testament to his innovative spirit, creativity, and perseverance.

As a distinguished musician, Harold has shared the stage with legendary artists. He has also imparted his knowledge as a college professor of communication, inspiring future generations of entertainment and education.

As the founder and owner of Chase Republic, a pioneering brand communication agency, Harold excels in cross-cultural advertising, marketing, and strategic partnerships. His agency has successfully collaborated with prominent brands and organizations and navigated diverse markets and audiences.

Harold's accomplishments extend beyond the entertainment industry. He has mastered two disciplines of martial arts, showcasing his dedication to discipline and self-improvement.

In recognition of his outstanding contributions, Harold has received a prestigious proclamation from the New York City Council, honoring his impact on the entertainment industry, education, and community development.

Through his work, Harold continues to inspire, educate, and empower others, cementing his legacy as a trailblazing leader and creative visionary.

Preface

"It's Beyond Words; It's The Art of Calculated Communication."

Unlock the secrets to effective communication and transform your personal and professional life. This insightful guide reveals the hidden codes of strategic communication, empowering you to navigate the complexities of human interaction with confidence and precision.

Starting with the foundational element of intrapersonal communication—the conversation within—you'll gain a deeper understanding of your inner dialogue, paving the way to self-actualization. From there, you'll learn how to harness the power of calculated communication to achieve success in all areas of your life.

Through the lens of emotional intelligence, you'll discover:

The distinction between leadership communication, powerless talk vs. the art of power talk, and its impact on personal and professional relationships.

The subtle yet persuasive language of seduction, from attraction to action.

What sets this book apart is the unique blend of theoretical foundations and real-life applications. As a seasoned entertainment executive, I draw upon my own experiences working with top talent, negotiating high-stakes deals, and navigating the complexities of the entertainment industry. You'll benefit from practical, behind-the-scenes examples that illustrate each concept, making it easier to apply these principles to your own life and career.

It's Beyond Words; It's The Art of Calculated Communication is more than just a book—it's a comprehensive toolkit for mastering the art of communication. Whether you're a business leader, entrepreneur, or simply looking to enhance your personal relationships, this book will equip you with the skills and strategies necessary to succeed in today's fast-paced, communication-driven world.

Introduction

Why Do We Study Communication, and What Is Communication?

Communication will always be the key to your personal and professional success. Your personal success can include friendships, romantic relationships, acquaintances, etc. Your professional success includes but is not limited to, your advancement at a job or career, and especially operating your own business.

It is important to state that communication and speaking are not synonymous!

When people hear the term *"communication,"* their perception of the word usually means *to talk* or *to speak* with someone. Communication is beyond your words. Words are simply the beginning of the journey to effective communication.

Communication involves connection more so than speaking.

Speaking with or to someone does not mean true communication is taking place. Without connection **(understanding, empathy, emotional intelligence)**, communication does not exist.

Communication is the sending and receiving of messages back and forth between senders and receivers, like a game of tennis.

- INTENT—executing your intent when communication is key in connection. If you do not intend to be harmful or disrespectful, you must make sure to apply emotional intelligence before you speak to the best of your ability because communication is irreversible.

Communication is irreversible.

Have you ever said or heard someone say, *"I take it back?"* Once you communicate, there is no *"taking it back."* You can apologize for a statement you made, but the statement itself cannot be erased. Once you send your message, that message now belongs to whoever received it. Just like in a game of tennis, once you serve the ball over the net, that ball is now in the court of the receiver and they can do as they choose with that tennis ball/message. The same rule will apply to messages sent via text messages or even messages released to media/social media. Once you hit send on a message or hit send on a post, that message now belongs to whoever reads it or sees it and can interpret the message however they like.

Noise can disrupt or prevent messages from connecting. It is a psychological barrier that exists inside the mind that prevents a sender's message from getting through.

Noise can be but is not limited to:

- Stereotypes
- Prejudices
- Preconceived notions
- Past experiences
- Assumptions

An example of noise and how it affects communication (connection) is to think of a statement you may hear people make regarding politicians. You may have often heard someone say that *"all politicians are liars."* This statement is subjective and not a fact so this is a form of noise. So, if a person running for Mayor is speaking with you to influence your vote, their message may not connect with you because the "noise" of **"all politicians are liars"** will ring louder in your mind than their actual words.

Although some politicians may be liars, it is not effective communication if you believe stereotypes about a person you have never met. The idea is not to turn the noise *off* but to turn the noise *down* just enough for the message to be heard. Giving someone the benefit of the doubt is a form of emotional intelligence.

How Do We Connect With Others?

The first step in connecting with others is understanding how we connect within ourselves.

Communication starts from within **(Intrapersonal Communication).** How you connect and understand yourself will allow you to properly connect and understand others.

Our words hold power. Be mindful of how you speak about yourself. If you constantly speak negatively or with doubt and uncertainty about yourself, you are more likely to invite those results into your life.

Even when you are faced with some level of adversity, you must speak life and strength inside of you, speak confidence and courage, and these results are more likely to happen for you.

When there is no way ... tell yourself you will find a way!

One of the important takeaways of this book is to understand the true meaning of communication. The illustration below highlights communication in its simplest form. As you progress through each chapter of the book, you will notice how we build on the illustration. The information in each chapter will serve as tools to add to the communication toolbox.

(illustration of communication)

This is communication in its simplest form: the sending and receiving of messages. As we journey through the chapters, you'll see how we build on this image.

This is an image of a person who is on the path to self-actualization, possessing intricate levels of intelligence.

Intrapersonal Intelligence –Mastering the Conversation Within

"Some people have a perception of who you are and what you are capable of. Once you exceed what they think you can do or accomplish, they say things like, 'Well, who does he/she think he/she is?'"

~ Oprah Winfrey

Interpersonal Communication

The key to fundraising is friend-raising. If you can't make friends, you can't make funds!

"Relationships are the true currency of business; the value is accepted where money isn't."

~ Harold Wilkerson

"The strongest foundations are built on friendship. Then the money follows that connection."

~ Unknown

"Your net worth depends on your network."

~ Tim Sanders

> "If there are ten people in a room, at least two possess a key to a door you need to open."
>
> ~ Harold Wilkerson

> "A good reputation is the best introduction you'll ever need."
>
> ~ Harold Wilkerson

Media & Manipulation

> "You are a manipulator."
> "I like to think of myself more as an outcome engineer."
>
> ~ J.R Ward

What Media Would Sound Like If It Could Speak

> "Whoever controls the media, the images, controls the culture."
>
> ~ Allen Ginsberg

> "Understanding the manipulation of media is equivalent to knowing how a magic trick works."
>
> ~ Harold Wilkerson

"In a world where information is power, the media decides who holds the key."

~ Harold Wilkerson

"The media will always be subjective and never objective. There is always a bias."

~ Harold Wilkerson

"Anything that is monetized has the potential to be corrupted."

~ Harold Wilkerson

"Whoever controls the media controls the mind."

~ Jim Morrison

Intercultural Communication

"Culture and race are not synonymous."

~ Harold Wilkerson

Culture is a choice, and your race isn't.

"Culture is learned; race is inherited—yet both are often mistaken for one another."

~ Harold Wilkerson

"Race is a social construct based on appearance; culture is a living, breathing expression of experience."

~ Unknown

"True intercultural intelligence lies in the ability to listen to the stories of others, even when they're told in a language you don't speak."

~ Harold Wilkerson

Emotional Intelligence and Communication

"It takes more than intelligence to act intelligently."

~ Fyodor Dostoyevsky

"The greatest power lies not in intellect, but in the ability to connect with and manage emotions—both yours and others."

~ Harold Wilkerson

"Emotional intelligence turns self-awareness into self-mastery and empathy into connection."

~ Harold Wilkerson

"Emotional intelligence isn't about avoiding difficult emotions, but about knowing how to navigate them with grace."

~ Unknown

"Emotional intelligence empowers us to turn our reactions into choices and our choices into growth."

~ Unknown

Leadership and Communication

"Leadership can exist without power, but there is no true power without the presence of leadership."

~ Harold Wilkerson

"It doesn't matter who draws the play as long as the team scores. Don't compete but complete."

~ Harold Wilkerson

"There are some people you can partner with and there are some you can employ. The skill is knowing the difference between the two. Always take a mental inventory of your personnel."

~ Harold Wilkerson

"If you're not making mistakes, you're not making decisions."

~ Catherine Cook

"I NOT ONLY USE ALL THE BRAINS THAT I HAVE, BUT ALL THAT I CAN BORROW."

~ Woodrow Wilson

Power and Communication

"VISION IS THE PRODUCT OF LEADERSHIP, AND POWER IS THEIR CURRENCY."

~ Harold Wilkerson

"It's better to ask for forgiveness than permission."

~ Grace Hopper

"Never say more than necessary."

~ Harold Wilkerson

"The words you use can either build or betray your worth."

~ Harold Wilkerson

"Speak from a place of authority and not an apology."

~ Unknown

"We have two ears and one mouth so that we can listen twice as much as we speak."

~ Epictetus

"The loudest voice in the room isn't always the one with the most power, but the one who knows how to communicate it."

~ Harold Wilkerson

"Never over-explain your actions."

~ Harold Wilkerson

Theories of Communication

Navigating the path from intrapersonal communication to leadership communication results in self-actualization—the realization or fulfillment of one's talents and potentialities, especially considered as a drive or need present in everyone.

Chapter 1:
Intrapersonal Intelligence

"The only way out is within."

~ Unknown

"Everything you wish to achieve is not as far as you think. It's as far as you can think."

~ Unknown

"In the midst of chaos, there is also opportunity."

~ Sun Tzu The Art of War

"In any given moment, we have two options: to step into growth or step back into safety."

~ Abraham Maslow

In the fall of 2016, my good friend Jeffery Atkins, BKA Ja-Rule, hired me as the Director of Talent for Fyre Media. FYRE is an acronym For Your Real Entertainment. The model of Fyre Media began as a high-profile talent acquisition platform/app for entertainers to receive offers for live entertainment opportunities directly from qualified buyers. My role in Fyre Media was to recruit and manage high-profile celebrities to utilize our service as well as engage with the buyers to execute their offers. I did not have involvement with the planning of the festival, but I will make mention of the festival and its planning in the Media Influence chapter of this book.

I will tell many stories from my time with Fyre to support the theories we are discussing, but it is essential that the stories I choose to tell coincide with the path of this book. There were exciting times during the early stages of Fyre. These times were filled with private jets, beach house parties in the Hamptons, and opportunities to build relationships with celebrity clients.

In the aftermath of May 2017, I found myself lost in the ashes and debris from Fyre Media, which the Fyre Festival caused. With the collapse of the company, I was unemployed with a sense of financial uncertainty. I learned that in the midst of chaos, there is also opportunity. This opportunity came in the form of entrepreneurship, and Chase Republic emerged! In a matter of two years, I was negotiating partnerships with Samsung, executing marketing activations with Major League Baseball, and structuring partnerships with The Brooklyn Nets.

This was my path to self-actualization, and it began with intrapersonal intelligence, The Conversation Within! Along with emotional intelligence, intrapersonal communication is an essential tool for navigating the path to self-actualization.

This book and the journey to self-actualization both begin with intrapersonal communication. This is equivalent to a film that begins by showing you the end of the movie as its first scene. When you are watching a movie that begins with the ending, as the plot unfolds, you come closer to the conclusion. Once you reach the ending scene, you receive an awakening or awareness of how it all connects. The end always connects to the beginning. Becoming the supreme version of yourself personally and professionally will begin with your intrapersonal communication.

The Conversation Within!

Intrapersonal communication or intrapersonal intelligence is defined as communication within the individual. It is an area of study that will be the foundation and the root of all areas of communication.

Your intrapersonal communication entails how you see yourself, your self-concept, your self-awareness, your ability to self-evaluate, and how you value yourself. How you feel about yourself will depict how you connect with others. It affects how you negotiate. It affects your belief in what you can achieve. Your intrapersonal communication can limit you or prepare you to be limitless.

Intrapersonal communication occurs when a person is communicating with others and when they are alone and thinking to themselves.

In any conversation between two people, there are actually four conversations taking place:

- Who you think you are (How you see yourself/what you think of yourself.)

> What you think they think you are (How does he or she see me/What does he or she think of me?)

> Who they think they are (How they see themselves.)

> Who they think you think they are (How they think you see them.)

To translate or offer clarity: The conversation you are having with them, the conversation you are having with yourself, the conversation they are having with you, and the conversation they are having with themselves.

This scenario can be applied to every encounter. It does not matter if you are on a first date with a superstar model or in a pitch meeting with the wealthiest, most famous individual.

If you ever find yourself in this situation, apply this strategy:

Do not think of their reputation or the myth of the person. If you communicate with them with that perception in your mind, you are at a disadvantage. You may become nervous, you may not appear to be confident, and you may be unable to communicate effectively. You will not have the presence of mind.

Think of them when they were not who they are now, when their insecurities may have been worn on their sleeves. Search for those insecurities. You may even go as far as zoning in on any physical insecurity they may have deep inside. Somewhere internally, they are still that person. When you train your mind to think in this way, you put yourself more at ease and are more confident in who you are, and you will be able to execute your agenda.

It is important to understand that the person you are sitting across from may also use this strategy against you. The best way for you to defend against this is to have a high frequency of intrapersonal intelligence, which will consist of understanding a self-concept and self-awareness. When you truly believe you are the person you are supposed to be, and your listeners also share that concept of you in their head, there is a high chance of executing your intentions from the conversation.

Example

If a CEO has a staff meeting to introduce a new agenda or an unfamiliar path for the company, the CEO's inner voice has been telling them that they are intelligent, they are an effective leader, and this is a good plan. When the staff also shares that concept of the CEO, their inner voice will say the same and the CEO now has a higher chance for the plan to be executed.

Example

I can recall when a friend first started to date a television star. He expressed his nervousness when thinking of being in her presence. My suggestion to him was to try not to spend too much time watching her TV shows and try not to spend too much time on her social media page. Although it is important to study and learn things about someone, you do not want to be overly engulfed in their world where you become fascinated with their reputation or celebrity. Too much admiration or fascination can cause you to be at a disadvantage because it may lead to hesitation in your communication. You may start to feel as if it is a privilege for you when it should be a mutual exchange.

The journey is to build a strong concept of yourself and position yourself to the point where that self-concept also exists in the minds of others.

Self-Concept

Self-concept is the central point of reference for how we communicate with others. It is the image that we have of ourselves. It is our individual feelings and thoughts about our behavior, strengths, capabilities, and characteristics. It is a mental picture of who you are. If you see yourself as a person with integrity, you are more likely to do what is right. If you feel you are an intelligent person, the chances are you will share ideas in a meeting or raise your hand in class. Self-concept is everything that encompasses the answer to the question, "Who am I?"

How Your Self-Concept Develops

Infants do not have a sense of self-concept. Self-concept gradually develops from the contact we have with significant people in our lives over a period of time. The parent or guardian that tells their child how smart they are will result in that child's performance and self-concept.

Self-concept tends to be more primitive or in its primary stages when people are young, but that is one of the most sensitive stages of the self-concept. As people age, their self-concept becomes much more detailed as people form a better idea of who they are. Our self-concept is defined by our relationships with significant people, siblings, friends, spouses, mentors. A person of significance saying the words, *"I believe in you,"* will transform to *"I BELIEVE IN ME."*

Sources of Self-Concept

- ➢ The self-image you have that others have, and they reveal that to you
- ➢ Comparisons you make between yourself and others
- ➢ Your culture
- ➢ Self-evaluations of your behavior. Without the ability to evaluate your own behavior, you will not fully connect with yourself, resulting in the inability to connect with others.

Self-Awareness

Self-awareness develops from self-concept. It is the extent to which you know yourself, your strengths, and your weaknesses.

Self-awareness is explained by four selves:

The Open Self

Represents the information about your behaviors, attitudes, feelings, and motivations that you and others know. Those attributes are what is on the surface.

The Blind Self

Represents all the things about you that others know but of which you are ignorant. This can include habits that you are not fully aware of, ways of behaving, and natural reactions.

It is important to take a deeper look into the Blind Self. You may have heard someone say to you, *"I know you better than you know yourself."* Although that comment may not possess much validity, there may be a percentage that is accurate. We all have attributes about us that we are not aware of but it can be clear to others. Usually, those attributes have an effect on our relationships.

To paint a picture of The Blind Self, think of a car traveling on a highway. When someone is driving a car, there is something called The Blind Spot. While they are traveling on a highway, they may not be aware of the car that is in their blind spot. Every other car on that highway can see the car adjacent to the traveler. When the traveler attempts to merge into another lane where the adjacent car sits in the blind spot, a car crash can take place. While the other cars that are traveling behind can clearly see both cars, they may start to honk their horn in a distasteful and aggressive manner to alert the traveler. Some of the other cars may even judge the traveler as a poor driver, but the traveler was not aware of what was inside the blind spot. Once the traveler sees the car, they can make the necessary adjustments to avoid a crash.

To connect the theory of the blind self and blind spot, I can offer a personal example. There may have been a time in my younger years when I was deemed by my close friends to be very selfish. I was not aware of how this trait was having a negative effect on my relationships. From an early age, I had to learn to fend for myself, and this created a terrible habit of being selfish. When my relationships were headed towards rocky waters, I would be told how selfish I was. After hearing this from a few close friends, I decided to self-evaluate and take accountability for how my selfish actions may have caused the deterioration of the relationship.

Now, I understand that being selfish can sit inside my blind self/blind spot. So, now that I am aware that I am behaving selfishly like the traveler on the highway noticing the car in its blind spot, I can make the necessary adjustments to avoid a communication crash.

The Hidden Self

Contains all that you know of yourself that you keep secret.

The Hidden Self does not mean you are keeping a secret. It means there are things about you that you would rather keep to yourself and not share with others.

The Unknown Self

Represents truths about yourself that neither you nor others know.

This can be revealed through temporary changes brought about by special conditions. The Unknown Self creates space for further self-discovery. It is important to embrace the idea of what is unknown about yourself. This concept allows you not to be 100% content with your current self. One should always challenge their abilities and push oneself to new limits.

Your Unknown Self can be revealed in the face of danger or tragedy. Your bravery can kick in and you may react in ways that can surprise you and others. Sometimes, you never know how strong you can be until all you have is strength to call on.

Confidence develops through self-awareness and recognition of one's strengths. Along with confidence, self-esteem grows, and one understands one's value.

When you unlock your internal strengths, you eliminate doubt and conquer fear. You not only accept challenges, but you seek them out. You see yourself as David in the story of David and Goliath and understand what is necessary to bring a giant to its knees.

Although supreme confidence is the greatest weapon you can arm yourself with, it is equally important to recognize your weaknesses. Once you identify your weaknesses, you must work on them. Being aware of your weaknesses or instabilities is a strength in itself. Those who choose to ignore this are more than likely exposing themselves to failure and disappointment.

In self-awareness, you must understand what is congruent and what is incongruent. Our self-concepts/awareness are not always accurately aligned with our reality or behavior. You must be able to self-evaluate. Some individuals have supreme confidence but a reputation for failure. Just because you drive cars, it doesn't necessarily mean you know how to build one on your own.

Congruence occurs when the person you think you are is actually aligned with your reality and behavior. Incongruence is when your reality and behavior do not match who you believe you are. YES, it is extremely important to have self-confidence. You should absolutely believe you are capable of building a car, but it is not enough to just simply believe you can do something. Along with that belief, you must identify your weaknesses and work on them, use your strengths, apply discipline and humility, seek knowledge, and be persistent and consistent. When all of these attributes are in harmony, your superpowers are unlocked, and then you reach self-actualization.

Intrapersonal communication plays a pivotal role in our journey to self-actualization. When we hear phrases like *"you're in your head"* or *"you're getting in your own way,"* it's often a reference to the mental barriers that hinder our progress. These obstacles can manifest regardless of our external circumstances, whether we're experiencing success or struggling with failure.

The key to overcoming these mental blocks lies in our ability to shift our mindset. We must cultivate a winning mentality, one that empowers us to persevere and push beyond our perceived limitations. The late Kobe Bryant famously coined the term *"Mamba Mentality,"* which embodies this concept of mental toughness.

By developing a growth mindset and harnessing our inner dialogue, we can unlock our full potential and achieve self-actualization. This journey requires discipline, resilience, and a deep understanding of our own thought patterns. As we master our intrapersonal communication, we'll be better equipped to navigate life's challenges and reach new heights of success.

(Draw the illustration with the added bubbles inside the mind of each stick figure to symbolize intrapersonal communication)

Applying the Theory

I can recall one day working on a particular deal for a company in Los Angeles. The company was looking to hire a certain celebrity, whom I will not mention, to host their holiday party. I had a close relationship with this artist's manager, so I figured this would be a seamless deal.

When I called my friend to explain the offer, I was surprised by his response. *"Hey, I'm hearing so many cool things about this Fyre Media company. Do you own the company, or do you work for them?"* I responded, *"No, I am an employee, but the pay is pretty good."* He then responded, *"Look, you know you are my friend, but you can keep the offer. If this was your company, I would do it. You, too, are smart! Stop calling me with opportunities that make everyone else rich but you!"*

Initially, I didn't understand why he wouldn't take the deal and work with me, but those words later sparked the fire in my eyes that I needed to guide my path to self-actualization.

DJ Khaled and Lenny S

I can remember the day Fyre folded, and I was hit with uncertainty about my financial future. When I was having lunch with a good friend and radio personality of iHeartMedia, similar words of encouragement rang out. *"You will never become who you are supposed to become if you don't take a chance on yourself."*

It was then that the idea of Chase Republic emerged. My intrapersonal communication screamed to me, *"You are unstoppable!"* I looked in the mirror and saw a lion in my eyes. With self-evaluation and self-awareness, I began to unlock my gifts and believe more in myself as an executive. I held myself accountable for my destiny. I stopped asking for what I needed and started demanding it instead. No matter the size of my company, I took pride in it being my company. It didn't matter the size of the ship; I was its captain, and I communicated as such.

Chase Republic quickly became a respected independent talent acquisition and brand communication agency. In three years, it earned me more economic gain than I have ever earned in my professional career. Transitioning from being financially lost after Fyre Media to controlling the room in meetings with corporations such as Major League Baseball, my growth is all credited to my intrapersonal intelligence.

The Conversation Within!

Self-Concept—A Student's Perspective

I really enjoyed all the topics discussed in class today, and I agreed with pretty much the whole lecture. I agree with the fact that what is going on inside of our mind is the most important part of connecting with others. How we feel about ourselves projects onto other people; if I am feeling depressed, angry, insecure, or have any negative feelings about myself, they are going to project onto the people I am trying to connect to. That is why most people say those who pick on others have something deeper going on within themselves. Someone just does not purposely try to make someone feel like shit unless they feel that way about themselves. Being able to look in the mirror and feel confident and beautiful and knowing that you have positive energy will allow you to connect with others more fluently. When we have a better self-concept, it allows us to feel more confident, which will radiate and allow others to feel invited to connect with us. Another important concept to understand is our "blind self," which essentially is comparable to the blind spot of a car. Other people can see what is in your blind spot, but you cannot; this correlates to the blind self because there are many attributes about yourself that you do not know you have. It is important that we are able to reflect on what people say about ourselves; this way, we are able to learn what characteristics are hidden in our blind spot, whether they be positive traits or negative traits. From this lecture, I learned a lot about how important it is to be able to connect and reflect on ourselves and others. Additionally, I learned the importance of strong intrapersonal connections and how they promote strong interpersonal connections.

~ Madison Haack (former student's introduction to an assigned paper on Intrapersonal Communication.)

Chapter 2: Interpersonal Communication

In June 2014, I was the road manager for Ja Rule at a show where he was performing alongside Jennifer Lopez. Backstage of this show is where I would meet Sam Hirsch. In 2014, Sam was the Executive Assistant to Brett Berish of Sovereign Brands. By the time Sam resigned in 2019 as Director of Marketing & Brand Partnerships, we had built a bond both as friends and business associates that would result in the execution of numerous brand partnership deals with marquee names in the entertainment industry, ultimately leading to the birth of Chase Republic.

Ja Rule

If you can't make friends, you can't make funds!

In August 2018, along with a handful of influential professionals in the entertainment world, we were hired by the government of Bermuda to curate an Influencer marketing activation surrounding Cup Match. Cup Match, one of Bermuda's biggest events of the year, takes place over two days in the Summer. The event is centered around a cricket match between two island rivals, St. George's and Somerset. While enjoying the festivities during a private dinner on the beach hosted by The Premier of Bermuda, David Burt, I was introduced to Fredrick Whitaker. Yaneley, a mutual friend and film & TV executive, introduced us with one statement, *"You two can make some money together."*

Fred and I did just that.

Rocsi Diaz, Fred Whitaker, Angela Yee, Chantel Cohen, Henrock, Shaffer

Interpersonal Communication

Interpersonal communication happens simultaneously between two or more people who attempt to mutually influence each other, usually to manage relationships.

To explain interpersonal communication and how it works, we must mention the first step or phase, which is the Uncertainty Reduction Theory.

Uncertainty Reduction Theory

UDR was initially introduced in 1975 by Charles R. Berger and Richard J. Calabrese.

The beginning of every relationship is met with uncertainty. All relationships begin with question marks. These question marks can range from something as simple as a person's favorite food, how they are with children, and how responsible they are with money to something much more intimate and intricate like this person's love language, how they deal with pressure, etc. We reduce uncertainty through knowledge and understanding of someone.

What are the ways we gain knowledge of someone?

Before reading this book, you may have thought getting to know someone or gaining knowledge of them just happens naturally. This is definitely true, but the UDR explains intentional methods we can use to do this.

When getting to know someone, do you ever find yourself saying, *"I like them, but I don't want to play this game?"*

Communication may not be a game, but there are definitely strategies that must be applied to reduce uncertainty when making attempts to connect with others. The sooner you realize this, the more leverage you will have in your attempts.

Charles R. Berger and Richard J. Calabrese spoke about three strategies:

- The Passive Strategy
- The Active Strategy
- The Interactive Strategy

The Passive Strategy

A person can disclose so much about themselves without ever uttering one word to you. A person is more likely to act their normal self when they aren't aware that they are being observed. It is important to mention that this is a method of strategy and not of moral ethics.

Example

- You may walk past a classmate in the hall and hear a joke they say to a friend. They are not aware you were paying attention. You quickly assessed them from the joke.

- You are in the parking lot of your job, and when a co-worker starts their car, you hear a song being played that tells you a little of their musical taste.

- During Casual Fridays at the office, a co-worker tends to always wear some sort of sports apparel.

- Inside the boss's office, there are pictures of their family from events. This may tell you something about their family dynamics or interests.

- You are in the beginning stages of dating, and you are invited over to the person's family home for the holidays. You will have an opportunity to view this person in their natural element.

- Viewing someone's social media page without their knowledge.

- Reviewing someone's playlist or musical choice can give you a glimpse of their personality.

- If someone is wearing a wedding ring or not.

- The kind of watch or jewelry a person is wearing.

All of what you observe is information being disclosed to you about this person that you can use later. In addition, you can find your point of entry into conversing with them.

You have two ears and one mouth. You should listen twice as much as you talk. If you listen long enough and have patience, a person will reveal everything you need to know about them. They will expose strengths, hidden weaknesses, intentions, characteristics, and traits that dwell inside their blind spots (blind self).

I can recall mentioning the active strategy to a class, and students would respond with the idea of this strategy sounding like something a stalker would do. I further explained to the class that when we are looking to get to know someone, we carry out these strategies subconsciously. Because you now know there is a term for it, you think something is cunning about it. So, I asked the class if they had ever explored a person's social media page without them knowing, or saw on their page that they have a friend in common, and asked that friend about them; the class agreed with the concept.

There is a key factor to remember while you are using the passive strategy. Just as you are utilizing these tactics, you are not exempt from these same strategies being used on you by someone gaining knowledge about you. Someone is always observing you. Once you are aware and fully digest this information, you will then understand how to paint the perception you want someone to see. This is called seduction and persuasive communication. This comes much later.

The Active Strategy

The Active Strategy is used when you ask others about the person you are interested in or set up a situation where you can observe the person without their knowledge.

- A company asking for your references for a job.
- A scout asking a coach about a player.
- Networking events: you ask a mutual friend about someone you met at an event to gather more information about them.
- You ask a friend to invite the person out for a social gathering.

Once the scenario is set up, we just observe, which is a passive strategy.

Interactive Strategy

We communicate directly with the person.

Sometimes, I hear some students mention they prefer the interactive strategy. I then point out the advantage you have when you use the strategies in order. Whatever the reason you are looking to get to know someone, gathering as much information as possible before you approach them will give you the edge when communicating with them.

The Social Penetration Theory

"The key to fundraising is friend-raising. If you can't make friends, then you can't raise funds."

This was the opening statement made by Professor Katie Ford to the class on the first day of Fundraising in Graduate School. Professor Ford elaborated by stating, *"Having the ability and skill to build relationships would determine the success of any business."*

Those words have stuck with me through every professional endeavor and have proved to be more practical than theoretical.

Social Penetration Theory, developed in 1973 by psychologists Irwin Altman and Dalmas Taylor, is a theory about the development of relational closeness.

How do relationships develop? How did someone who once was a stranger become a great friend? How did you develop an intimate connection with someone? Why are you closer to one person than another?

Professional and personal relationships may differ in cost and rewards, but the inception of all relationships is the same. Regardless of nature, all relationships explore the same stages. The initial development stage of any relationship is called the Social Penetration Theory.

To interpret the theory, it is best to visualize the concept of using your social behavior or social skills to penetrate the natural shell or wall that exists when you first meet someone.

Relationships can progress from superficial to intimate. The theory states that relationships begin, deepen, and become closer through self-disclosure.

Self-Disclosure

Self-disclosure is sharing with someone information about you that helps them understand who you are. This may include thoughts, feelings, aspirations, goals, failures, successes, fears, and dreams, as well as one's likes, dislikes, and favorites.

Besides wanting a person to understand who we are, one of the reasons we share things about ourselves is because we want the receiver to share information about them so we can become closer. When you disclose information about yourself, you hope for quality feedback when the receiver is disclosing information about themselves. When you are sharing with someone something as simple as your drink of choice, you will hope they respond with their drink of choice and not a generic, *"Oh, that's nice."* Similarly, if you are sharing your aspirations, and goals, you would hope for a genuine response along with what *their* goals and aspirations are.

The process of disclosing information about yourself can happen intentionally or unintentionally. Since it is possible for you to disclose information about yourself subconsciously, it is very important to be intimately familiar with all forms of your communication. The way you dress, your body language, your natural reactions, immediate responses—all of these things can tell someone something about you that you possibly didn't mean to share.

The counter concept is the idea that you can purposefully make your communication seem unintentional, but you are fully aware of your agenda. An example of this is a time I was asked to attend a networking event hosted by an executive of Def Jam Records. Although this executive and I were familiar with one another, we did not have a relationship. I was looking to build a relationship by attending her event. I was aware that she was a part of the Alpha Kappa Alpha, and their sorority colors are pink and green. I decided to wear a pink Ralph Lauren polo shirt that displayed a green polo logo. When I came face to face to greet her, the first words she spoke were, *"I love this color on you."* This is all I needed to begin a conversation.

The power of being intimately familiar with unintentional self-disclosure is that you become aware when someone else is disclosing information about themselves unintentionally. A logo on a hat, facial expressions, the color of their tie, the scent of perfume or cologne, their body language, and what they choose to share on social media all contribute to how a person learns about another. Although these examples are more ambiguous than direct, one should still be observant and aware of them.

Stages of Self-Disclosure

Altman and Taylor first described the process of self-disclosure as peeling back the layers of an onion. Personalities have layers. It starts from the outside (what the public sees) all the way to the core of what is private. When people disclose information about themselves, they are peeling their layers. Once the layers peel, they cannot put them back on. To elaborate, once a person shows you their true self, it is impossible for them to disguise it to you. The idea is to use your self-disclosure to encourage someone to peel back their layers and open up to you.

Self-disclosure creates a connection, and through the consistent connection, the relationship expands to a deeper level. When disclosure diminishes, connection weakens, and the idea of the relationship progressing will be at risk. A quality connection is key in all relationship building. It is imperative to find ways to stay connected. If this is a professional relationship, something as simple as remembering a birthday or something significant to the person are ways the relationship has a chance to expand past the current level.

Think of a relationship that is largely based on a physical connection and very little self-disclosure. Once either individual is exposed to another person with a deeper sharing connection and a high degree of self-disclosure is taking place, the previous relationship may not proceed past the current level and will possibly end.

This theory can also be applied in business. People would rather do business with those they like, trust, and connect with. In some professional relationships, simply doing business does not garner connection. It can just be transactional. A person who has a stronger connection and trust, and has proven to be a good business partner will have a better chance at a long-term commitment. There is no worth in simply knowing someone or being familiar; the value is in how they know you and how you know them.

1. Orientation Stage

This stage is also known as the *"small talk"* or *"first impression"* stage.

Communicators become acquainted by observing mannerisms and personal dress and by exchanging non-intimate information about themselves.

2. Exploratory Affective Stage

Communicators begin to reveal more about themselves. Deeply personal information is withheld. Casual friendships develop at this stage, and most relationships stay at this level.

3. **Affective Stage**

Communicators begin to disclose personal and private matters. Personal ways of speaking, or unconventional language, are allowed to come through. They feel comfortable enough to argue or criticize each other. You aim to get the communicator to open up, identify their insecurities, and try to strengthen them.

Communicators are very uncomfortable exposing or disclosing their vulnerabilities. By self-disclosing and exposing your vulnerability, you can attempt to get them to share theirs.

4. **Stable Stage**

The people share a relationship in which disclosure is open and comfortable. They can predict how the other person will react to certain types of information.

5. **Depenetration**

This occurs when one or both communicators perceive that the cost of self-disclosure outweighs its benefits. There may not be any quality feedback, and trust might be questioned. Communicators withdraw from self-disclosure and possibly end the relationship.

Conversation and Listening

Striking and carrying a conversation with a stranger can be very difficult. Of course, an introduction from a mutual acquaintance allows a head start in the initial conversation process. Although association and familiarity are valuable currencies, they may not be available at the moment.

Striking a conversation with a stranger can be difficult, but with effective communication strategies, you can have the opportunity to turn a stranger into a long-lasting acquaintance.

Here are some tips you should follow when you are looking to strike up a conversation:

Confidence

Confidence is a characteristic that dwells inside your intrapersonal intelligence.

In any room, no matter the caliber of people inside, you must feel as if you belong there. That confidence will shine bright for all to see and will be your best weapon to chip away at a possible defensive communicative wall.

Confidence is alluring, but it's important to state that confidence and humility should be combined. Cockiness or conceit will not get you anywhere.

How to Execute

Before you engage in any conversation, you should scan the room and observe the person you are planning to engage from a distance. A person is more likely to display things about themselves when they are self-monitored or when they do not feel someone is observing them. (Uncertainty Reduction Theory)

Look for your openings. In some circumstances, you may not be able to accomplish what you set out to in one encounter. It may require you to be in their presence more. You must have patience and allow the opportunity to give an opening. Sometimes, just a simple greeting or being introduced is enough to plant a seed for the next encounter. It will usually take a minimum of two encounters for those seeds to settle in.

Let the game come to you.

This is a sports reference that many NBA coaches tell their players in big games. Don't be anxious; trust who you are, trust in your abilities, and let the game come to you.

Don't look to score 50 points with one basket. When you allow your natural skills to lead and not be over-anxious, everything will flow naturally, and you will create and find your moments to score.

An example of this is in 2022, when I was invited by Ron Robinson, a friend/film director, to be on the set of a film called "Russ and Drew," starring Meagan Good and Terence J. By this time, I had already established a prior professional and personal relationship with Meagan, Terrence, and pretty much all of the producers on this film. I saw this as an opportunity to reinforce and strengthen my relationship with

Meagan, Terrence, and some of the cast through casual but strategic conversation.

The night before going to the set, I found myself anxious to arrive and execute my goals. I had to remind myself *to "let the game come to me."* I told myself not to abandon my skills to communicate and build relationships, to trust in my abilities, and to look for my moments to score and not force any shots.

Once I was able to settle in and allow the game to flow, I was able to execute my goals. I not only was able to have effective and quality moments with everyone, but I was also able to establish a new relationship with Paige Hurd, one of the co-stars of the film. Paige and I went on to build a solid professional relationship years after. I scored 50 points by letting the game come to me naturally and not forcing my communication.

Meagan Good

Paige Hurd

Farming and Hunting

"Too many individuals network with the purpose of accomplishing an immediate goal. That's not networking; that's selling."

~ Unknown

When discussing the use of the social penetration theory while building professional relationships, networking is a key skill to possess. You may have heard the saying, *"Your net worth depends on your network."* If there are ten people in a room, at least two possess a key to a door you need to open. The skill is in identifying who those two people are. Many people do not have effective networking skills. These individuals have a pattern where they will attend events, have conversations with people, and exchange contact information, but the relationships never develop. To be fair, not every encounter will lead to a desired end, but one must know the science of networking or building relationships is equivalent to farming and hunting.

"To be successful, you have to be able to relate to people; they have to be satisfied with your personality to be able to do business with you and to build a relationship with mutual trust."

~ George Ross

Corey Smith, VP of DEI, LVMH

Gena Smith, Chief HR Officer, LVMH

Harold Wilkerson, Chase Republic

A relationship that involves hunting is when you can immediately identify the benefit of connecting with this person, and you look to execute your goal. For example, suppose you have a nonprofit organization, and you are invited to an event where some of the guests can potentially become donors to your organization. In that case, you know exactly how you can benefit from having a relationship, and they are clear on how they can benefit from you.

This applies in many forms. If you are an artist and you have an opportunity to meet a record exec, or if you are a programmer with a new app and you meet a potential investor. The concept is called *hunting* because you identify the prey, go for a kill, and are looking for an immediate benefit. This immediate benefit can come in the form of a meeting, a conference call, or some sort of direction of where the relationship can land.

> *"A really important part of networking is actually about what you bring to the table–not just what you want to get out of it. Contribution is a big part of networking success."*
>
> ~ Gina Romero

A relationship that involves farming requires patience, discipline, and vision. These particular relationships take time to grow. The benefit of the connection isn't as clear. Your patience will be applied as you plant the seeds, water, and feed the relationship. The seeds are planted by going through some of the layers of the social penetration theory. You are getting to know the person, building trust, staying connected, creating opportunities for the person to get to know you. Your discipline is applied when you are not forcing an outcome. You have a vision of where the relationship can possibly lead to or land. Staying consistent and persistent is important. As the planted seeds mature into fruit, you reap the benefits.

"The new form of networking is not about climbing a ladder to success; it's about collaboration, co-creation, partnerships, and long-term values-based relationships."

~ Porter Gale

"Hard Rock Hotel international / Chase Republic launching live betting and Roulette at the Guitar Hotel in Hollywood, FL"

Chantel Cohen, Harold Wilkerson, Dwyane Wade, Ja Rule, and Fat Joe.

A farming relationship isn't transactional. It is a cycle that will repeat as long as the relationship feels mutually beneficial.

"Those that win in farming a relationship give first, give generously, and give often."

~ Harold Wilkerson

Ice Cube

Angela Yee

DJ Envy & Harold Wilkerson

Farming Relationships

An example of a farming relationship is how my partnership with The Brooklyn Nets began. My connection to The Nets started when a client who worked for Red Bull was hosting a company night out and extended an invitation for me to attend The Nets vs. Knicks in a box suite at the Barclays Center. During the game, I would be introduced to Emmanual Jacobo, VP of Sales for the Barclay Center. While enjoying the game and engaging in casual conversation, Manny and I learned we had a few things in common. We were both raised in the same area in the Bronx. We exchanged contact information and kept in touch. Whenever I wanted to attend a game and host a client, Manny would provide me with floor seats. To show my gratitude for the floor seats, I would send thank-you gifts to Manny's office. The gifts would range from cases of champagne to apparel. After just two years of Manny and me farming a relationship that began with a game and floor seats, I found myself negotiating partnerships with the Brooklyn Nets upper executive office, also developing a relationship with the CEO, Oliver Weisberg, and former CRO, Mike Zadvosky.

> *"What makes farming work is that it sets up win-win situations in which all parties involved get to take something home. It is a sharing process. Until you understand that, you won't have much of a network."*
>
> ~ Harold Wilkerson

A Farming Scenario

3/30/24

On a beautiful spring afternoon in Soho, I was having brunch in a popular restaurant with my friend Herbert Rice and my friend/client Jarule.

As we were enjoying our meal, Jennifer Lopez and her husband, Ben Affleck, walked in. When they noticed us, Jen and Ben walked towards our table to greet us. Ja introduced us to Jen and Ben, and we all exchanged pleasantries. Jen and Ben sat at a table away from us but in our viewing distance. Ironically enough, a few weeks before this moment in the restaurant, Ja's team and Jen's team discussed adding him to Jen's upcoming tour, but neither side could agree on terms. It's important to state here that Ja and Jen never spoke to one another directly about the tour; only their management engaged in the negotiations.

As we were finishing our meal, I suggested to Ja that he extend a communication olive branch and secretly pay for Jen and Ben's meal as we exited the restaurant. According to my plan, Jen would be very appreciative of the gesture and would call Ja personally to thank him. Once she would do that, he would have a gracious point of introduction to further develop their relationship and personally work out whatever details were preventing them from touring together. Needless to say, Ja declined my suggestion. Ja did make a great point by mentioning it may be inappropriate for a table of three men to offer to pay for the meal of a woman who sat with her husband and sister.

What would you have done?

"The size of your network doesn't matter – it is the quality of your network that counts."

~ Unknown

Social Capital

When you are networking, you are building your social capital. Social Capital is the network of relationships you have among people who may work in your particular industry. Social Capital is your resource. To conceptualize it, think of a country that is rich with oil or gold as its natural resources. These resources are valuable to their country and other countries. Your social capital is some of your "natural resources."

This is part of what makes you valuable to others. You should treat your resources the same as a country treats theirs. Resources should never be given away for free. There is always a barter system, but it is extremely important to know that within a bartering system, not all rewards are economic. *Translation:* You will miss out on many opportunities, thinking that every opportunity must result in a cash reward. This is the epitome of farming!

"LVMH / Chase Republic: Art Basel"

Harold Wilkerson, Corey Smith, Gena Smith, and Jacques Evans.

Ecosystems

As you build up your social capital, it is important to establish ecosystems. In scientific terms, an ecosystem is a geographic area where plants, animals, and other organisms, as well as weather and landscape, work together to form a bubble of life. Every factor in an ecosystem depends on every other factor, either directly or indirectly, for its survival. Creating ecosystems in professional relationships will aid in economic growth.

For example, my social capital (resources) may consist of entertainers in the music field. My colleague Fred Whitaker's social capital may consist of actors and actresses. Another colleague of mine, Saedra Bracy, works for an advertising agency. Her social capital consists of several brands and corporations. These brands are looking to partner with artists, actors, and entertainers.

Together with trust, efficiency, and consistency, an ecosystem is created. Each person involved depends on one another for business to circulate. When Saedra meets with brands at her agency that are looking to partner with some form of talent to advertise their brand, Saedra contacts my agency for the talent. If, for any reason, I cannot deliver the talent requested, I contact Fred at his agency. Between the two of us, talent gets delivered, and a deal is done.

It is very important to reiterate that an ecosystem cannot exist without trust.

The Web of Affiliation

The web of affliction is a community of individuals who are connected in some form or another, but their relation to one another is not always obvious. This is equivalent to having relatives. Everyone belongs to the web. There is power in the web if used effectively, but not understanding the power of the web of affiliation can be dramatically harmful to you. Making friends with one person can open you up to their web of affiliation, but making enemies with a person can also expose you to dangers that might not be obvious to you.

The Dangers of the Web

An example of the dangers would be a time I can recall a particular hip-hop artist getting into an altercation with a radio DJ. When this DJ did not play the artist's music at a venue, the artist decided to post a disrespectful comment about the DJ on social media. The remarks were harsh and circulated throughout the music industry. The circulation of the post landed on the DJ's web of affiliation. In a matter of two weeks, the artist's music stopped being played in over 90 markets in the country. Bloggers released social media posts about the artist that impacted his sales. In a matter of six months, he was dropped from his record label.

The Power of the Web

An example of the power of the web would be my relationship with Fred Whitaker, manager to the stars. Once Fred and I met in Bermuda during Cup Match, we quickly began to build a friendship and professional relationship. Our relationship was a mixture of farming and hunting. It was clear that we both understood our connection would be mutually beneficial. Some of Fred's affiliates were obvious to me, while others were unknown.

When I was creating an influencer marketing campaign for Major League Baseball's Jackie Robinson's annual celebration, I called Fred to hire his exclusive client, actor Terrence J. MLB. Chase Republic created gift boxes that held an exclusive Jackie Robinson jersey along with a plaque of recognition to send to the listed influencers to post on their social media. When I called Fred to have him provide me with his client's address, he asked if I had an additional gift box. Although each box was accounted for, we made the arrangements. When the day arrived for the influencers to post their gift box honoring Jackie Robinson Day, not only did Terrence J. post but unexpectedly, actor and superstar Michael B. Jordan did as well. Michael B. Jordan was part of Fred's web of affiliation.

The Trojan Horse Theory

The Trojan Horse Theory is a story from the Trojan War about the deception tactic the Greeks used to enter the independent city of Troy and win the long-fought war. The City itself was constructed with cut limestone walls that were 15 feet thick, rose to a height of more than 17 feet, and was equipped with watchtowers. Troy's architecture was designed to keep their enemies on the outside and make it almost impossible for their arrows to ascend over the walls.

After years of unsuccessful attempts to invade Troy, the Greeks devised the Trojan Horse strategy. The Greeks built an enormous wooden Trojan horse that they would leave at the gates of Troy and pretend to sail away. The soldiers of Troy accepted the wooden horse as a sign of victory. They opened the gates of Troy and brought the horse inside. Unbeknownst to them, inside the wooden horse hid the Greek's greatest warriors. When night fell, the Greek soldiers that were inside the Trojan Horse emerged and burned the city of Troy to ashes and won the war.

The Application

The only true way to alter, destroy, improve, or influence is from the inside. This scenario can be applied to personal and professional relationships. No one person or organization is exempt from the Trojan Horse theory. From a personal relationship standpoint, the only way a person can truly love you or hurt you is if this person navigates through the communication channels to become close to you.

As I am sure you've heard the saying, *"It is the ones closest to you that can do the most harm,"* this is equally true when someone loves you. Love is an inside job.

To implement effective change inside an organization, you must be inside the organization. While an organization's complaints or boycotts garner attention, those complaints can only transform into a changed environment from the inside.

A Trojan Horse can also come in the form of an associate who works for a specific company with which you are looking to do some sort of business. Once you establish a strong relationship with that individual, that person will become your counterpart within that organization. Your Trojan Horse is an ally that also has the trust of your "enemy"—not the enemy in its literal sense, but the individual or organization you look to gain access to.

Another example of a Trojan Horse is when the FBI uses undercover agents to infiltrate criminal organizations.

Now, the key to applying this theory is to identify what one should use as its Trojan Horse. The Greeks used a wooden Trojan Horse that symbolized the city of Troy. It was a gift that flattered the Trojans. Half the battle of knowing what your Trojan Horse would be is understanding what would appeal to your target. Once you have identified your Trojan Horse and it has been accepted, you then apply strategy, patience, and precision to your execution.

Chapter 3: Intercultural Communication

What Culture Means to Me

When I was in 7th grade, Donald Trump won the election to be President of the United States.

As an extremely tanned, hairy-armed, messy-haired girl, this was my worst nightmare. All my life, I had been indifferent to my heritage. I neither hated nor loved it. I knew I was Mexican, and I knew being Mexican came with its own sets of negative stereotypes. I knew this because I had been living with a housekeeping mother and a construction-working dad. Throughout my whole 7th-grade experience, I only remember the shame I felt every single day to have to walk outside knowing that I was Mexican.

People would ask me where my family was from, and I would tell them that I was Venezuelan as a joke and never directly answer their questions. It angered me that everyone thought we were *"stealing their jobs"* and that we were *"criminals"* just because a white American man said so. I wish they would have taken the time to get to know us, learn about our country, and display cultural sensitivity.

~ Ashley Davila Gonzalez (a former student's introduction to an assigned paper on culture and communication)

Culture

This chapter has been the longest chapter for me to begin writing. I had almost considered leaving this chapter out of the book because thoughts surrounding culture and its true meanings are sensitive topics. The discussion on culture is multi-layered, and no matter where I begin this chapter, something will be said about what's missing.

Whenever it came time to cover culture and communication in the classroom, I would first ask the students, *"How do you define culture?"* After hearing everyone's ideas of how they define culture, ranging from religion, language, ways of life, music, art, fashion, food, customs, beliefs, values, principles, ways of thinking, traditions, which are all correct when describing culture, I would then say, *"Culture is a specialized lifestyle of a group of people that is passed down from one generation to the next by communication and not through genes."*

Then, I would tell them that culture is not synonymous with race. Culture and race are different. Some students would appear to be perplexed by the statement. I would then remind them of their answers when I proposed the question, and no one mentioned race as an attribute of culture. As we peeled back more layers in intercultural communication, the understanding would become clear that culture is a choice and your race isn't.

As my colleague and Wieden and Kennedy executive Marcus Collins mentions in his book *For The Culture*, *"Culture is one of those words that is often used but seldom understood. This is not surprisingly considering both the intangible nature of culture and our relatively loose use of it in our everyday lives. Culture is the program for everyday living, like the programming code that makes up an operating system, providing a navigable user experience."*

Cultural Sensitivity

Cultural sensitivity is an attitude and way of behaving in which one is aware of and acknowledges cultural differences. Having a high sense of cultural sensitivity can be one of the many keys to personal and professional success.

Without cultural sensitivity, there can be no effective interpersonal communication between people who are different in gender, race, or nationality. You must be mindful of the cultural differences between yourself and others. It is essential to have cultural sensitivity in order to navigate a diverse environment.

Cultural sensitivity is a part of all communication. The messages we send and receive all originate with values, beliefs, ways of life, and ways of understanding; therefore, they need to be considered in any full communication analysis.

The two most important aspects of cultural sensitivity are cultural relativism and ethnocentrism.

Cultural Relativism

Cultural relativism is the idea/theory that all cultures are different and that no culture is either superior or inferior to any other. Possessing this ideology allows you to communicate with others with an open mind. Under cultural relativism, one will not believe people should fully assimilate and leave their native culture behind and adapt to their new culture.

Understanding cultural relativism means having a perspective that values cultural diversity.

Acculturation and Assimilation vs. Appropriation

Acculturation, assimilation, and appropriation are sensitive and possibly misunderstood concepts concerning culture and communication.

Acculturation is defined as the ways in which one may experience or learn a culture different from one's own. Assimilation takes place when you begin to appreciate the new culture you are learning, and now aspects of this culture also become a way of life for you.

An Example of Acculturation and Assimilation - Jeremy Lin and Kenyon Martin

In 2017, Kenyon Martin, a former NBA player, made some not-so-nice remarks regarding the hairstyle of a current NBA player, Jeremy Lin. Kenyon Martin, who is African American, commented on the hairstyle of Jeremy Lin, who is of Taiwanese-American descent.

Kenyon Martin's Remarks

"Do I need to remind this damn boy that his last name is Lin? Like, come on, man. Let's stop this, man, with these people. Like, there's no way possible he would've made it on one of our teams with that bull**** going on on his head. Come on, man. Somebody really needs to tell him, like, 'All right, bro, we get it; you want to be black.' Like, we get it. But the last name is Lin, all right." ~ Kenyon Martin

Jeremy Lin's Response

"Hey, man. It's all good. You don't have to like my hair, and definitely entitled to your opinion. Actually, I'm legit grateful you sharin' it [to be honest]. At the end of the day, I appreciate that I have dreads and you have Chinese tattoos [because] it's a sign of respect. And I think as minorities, the more we appreciate each other's cultures, the more we influence mainstream society." ~ Jeremy Lin

Ethnocentrism

Ethnocentrism is the tendency to see others and their behaviors through your own cultural filters. It's the tendency to evaluate the values and beliefs of your own culture as superior. To achieve effective interpersonal communication, you need to see yourself and others as different but neither as inferior nor superior.

This can be a common issue that many have. Highly ethnocentric people think that other cultures should be more like theirs. Once you identify this as a conflict with an interpersonal connection, you will have more awareness of when this is taking place and how to decrease your level of ethnocentrism.

An Example

Attending a potluck at your office may help you pinpoint ethnocentrism. If you work in a diverse environment, there is a high chance that some of the food served will be different from what you may be used to culturally.

Reacting negatively or inappropriately to a prepared dish from another culture can be insulting and affect your professional and personal relationships. Just because the dish might look, smell, or taste different from the food of your culture does not mean that your food is better; it means that it is different.

Similarly, criticizing someone's music, language, clothing, religion, and way of life in comparison to your own is another example of ethnocentrism.

This theory applies to all aspects of culture.

Low Degree of Ethnocentrism

- Treats others as equals
- Evaluates other ways of doing things
- Open-minded and not influenced by the media's negative stereotypical images

High Degree of Ethnocentrism

- Avoids and limits interpersonal interaction with others, prefers to only interact with others from the same race and culture
- Belittles others who are not of the same culture
- Views own culture as superior to other cultures

~ Student's Reflection Paper on Culture and Communication

Last week, we began our discussion on culture and communication. I've always partly known what *culture* means, but if someone asked me to describe it before last week, I probably would've just listed a few topics mentioned in class, such as music, art, food, etc. This is because culture is so all-encompassing. How can we be able to just define it in a few words?

However, we did end up learning a definition of this word thanks to you, Professor, who has been doing this for a long time. Culture is a specialized lifestyle of a group of people that is passed down to generations through communication.

Now, this might seem self-explanatory, but I personally have never heard an actual definition of *culture*. I have found this definition helpful as I can now compartmentalize how culture works instead of it just being this constant entity that I know exists within groups of people.

Something we've addressed in class is why it is important to know all this information in a communications course. Culture is one of the biggest lenses through which an individual communicates. These beliefs, morals, opinions, likes and dislikes, etc., have been consistently influencing every second of oneself since birth. How could something like this not affect how we communicate with others? Culture may not be an aspect of communication that we are aware of when connecting with other people, but once we put a name and a definition to it, we see how much it impacts communication.

Preconceived notions and stereotypes can be developed by a culture, which can, in turn, change how individuals, for example, introduce themselves to a new person of another culture for the first time. They may have heard something negative about this culture through their own culture, and this will reflect in the way they speak or interact with this person if they truly believe it.

Becoming more culturally aware, and understanding cultural relativism is the number one way to make sure culture isn't standing in the way of effective communication. An individual can make an effort to think more about or find more information when encountering something different from their culture. I'm not saying people have to go studying and memorizing ways to be respectful of another culture, but just knowing about differences and recognizing there are things you might not get right away is the way to start being culturally sensitive. Once a person understands that no culture is above another, that they are just simply different, they can work to be aware of this as they are communicating with someone who belongs to another culture.

Student Amanie DiSieno's Reflection Paper on Intercultural Communication

After the past two classes, I found a deeper significance in intercultural communication than I have ever been able to before, for two reasons: modern-day connections and enlightenment from other students' discussions in class. I have to preface by saying that I don't necessarily agree with many aspects or opinions that align with today's "woke culture." However, I believe in respecting all people. I believe that there is beauty in our differences, and if everyone tried to understand one another rather than judge, we'd have a more well-rounded society.

After discussing the importance of the tools in our intracultural toolbox—specifically acculturation and assimilation—I was able to make real-world connections, furthering my interest in the topic. Due to the prominence of "woke culture" in America today—not to be confused with the original definition of awareness of racial injustice during the early 1900s—there is a lack of concrete understanding of what is considered appropriation of culture and acculturation. To better understand my point, appropriation is defined as *the action of exclusively taking something,* whereas *acculturation,* as defined in class, is *the way you experience and learn a new culture.*

The reason I bring up "woke culture" is because I feel as though many of the beliefs that align with today's "woke culture" tend to label many instances of acculturation as appropriation. I found this idea most supported by the Jeremy Lin story discussed in class. According to the article that was read, Jeremy Lin, a Taiwanese-American basketball player, had decided to wear dreads, which is typically a Black American hairstyle. Kenyon Martin, a former basketball player, decided to tweet that Lin needed to "...stop this... We get it, you want to be black..." to which Lin had responded that it was a sign of appreciation, similar to the Chinese tattoos Martin had on his body. The significance of this story, especially in the midst of society today, is that an increasing number of people spark controversies due to the mistaken definition of appropriation. Lin never stole or took the dread hairstyle away from Black American culture; he simply acculturated it due to the environment and experiences he had grown up with.

Another example to support my idea is one that happened in class. During a class discussion, a student had shared her own experiences with her family and their culture. She had mentioned that her father, mother, and grandparents all had different beliefs and traditions, but they never forced her to choose one of their own and instead educated her so that when the time was right, she'd be able to decide what beliefs aligned with her the most. As we discussed cultural sensitivity, I realized her family had been incredibly culturally sensitive to each other, respecting the differences that they may have had. However, another student commented on her story and called this phenomenon *"culture vulturing."* According to her definition, a *"culture vulture"* is someone who steals people's culture, coincidentally, an incredibly similar definition to appropriation. However, the original student never said she stole anyone's culture. In fact, she had been raised within multiple different cultures, expanding her own cultural sensitivity and cultural relativism.

Today, many people want to blame others for stealing, taking, or appropriating cultures that aren't theirs, not to say that this doesn't happen because it does. However, this is creating a huge disconnect in society, especially when acculturation is being mistaken, due to ignorance, as appropriation or *"culture vulturing."*

Being socially aware of injustices towards certain groups is incredibly beneficial as an individual and a society. However, instead of victimizing oneself and accusing others of stealing, it's important to educate and constantly learn about different people and cultures. Jeremy Lin couldn't have said it better, *"It's easy to take things that we enjoy from other cultures — that's one of the coolest things about a melting-pot society like ours... we have to be careful that taking doesn't become all we do. With all the division in our society right now, we need to talk to each other more than ever."*

Chapter 4:
Media & Manipulation

"You are a manipulator."

"I like to think of myself more as an outcome engineer."

~ J.R Ward

"Whoever controls the media, the images, controls the culture."

~ Allen Ginsberg

On December 27, 1999, Moses Michael Levi Barrow, better known by his stage name Shyne, a hip-hop recording artist and protégé of Sean P. Diddy Combs, discharged a firearm inside a nightclub in Times Square, injuring three people. Shyne was convicted in March 2001 on two counts of assault, reckless endangerment, and gun possession.

How does this relate to media and manipulation? Is hip-hop music a hero or a villain? Understanding the manipulation of media is equivalent to knowing how a magic trick works.

Media

As described in an article by Market Business News, media refers to "the communication channels through which we distribute news, music, movies, education, promotional messages, and other data."

Media is how we receive information. When reading this segment, it will be imperative to realize that media includes but is not limited to the following: physical and online newspapers and magazines, television, the news, billboards, telephone, the internet, the music you listen to, the movies you watch, sitcoms, reality shows, commercials, your social media page, the Bible, this book you are reading.

Under the Influence

When discussing media's influence and manipulation, it is important to understand that theories only offer an intuitive vantage point that supports a subjective scope rather than an objective one. Media will always be subjective and never objective. There is always a bias. To further explain, every media outlet has its own bias. That bias can be driven by, but is not limited to, political, economic, or personal gain. Anything that can be monetized has the potential to be corrupted, and media is no exception. If you do not understand the strategic maneuvers in the media, you may not recognize the agenda. The bias and the media's subjective views will transfer into the information and imagery you receive and will be strategically placed.

On the topic of media and influence, a psychological component must be considered. What triggers the brain?

What causes curiosity to result in action? I have mentioned in all my classes that psychology and communication are parallel. What affects the mind will affect the action.

In some aspects, I like to think of the media as the wizard of OZ—someone who does not exist but influences and manipulates our wants and needs on this yellow brick road of life.

Media can create or feed into our passions, our fears, our insecurities, and our fantasies. Media tells us who we are, who we should be, and what we should be afraid of. It influences what we eat, what we drink, and what we wear. It can influence how we define beauty, how we define success, or our social status. Media can shape your identity.

Ways Media Influences Society

In my attempt to make this theory relatable, I offer examples of how so many are influenced by the media.

Have you ever looked at someone and said to yourself, "Wow, he or she looks like a serial killer?" Where did this thought originate? Was it a movie you watched? Was it a news channel, an article, a book? Whichever media outlet influenced this thought, the image resonated with you when you came in contact with someone who resembled that image. You may have tried to avoid that person, you may have treated them differently, or you may have even tried to notify authorities.

Allowing the media to influence your actions by subscribing to negative stereotypes can cause conflict. I am not asking for you to be naive. I am asking for you to apply emotional intelligence in your interactions and be aware of the media's influence on your thoughts. This concept applies to every stereotype of every race, religion, and culture. The media can be responsible for creating these stereotypes.

Film and TV

In regards to film and television, *A Different World,* (a spinoff sitcom from The Cosby Show) would be the greatest influence for me to attend college. *A Different World* depicts the life of students at Hillman College, a fictional historically black college in Virginia. It was inspired by student life at historically black colleges and universities. The characters' backgrounds on the show were relatable in many ways. This show made college life fun, inspiring, and something you wanted to be a part of. Before *A Different World,* I would not have had the opportunity to see or hear what college life could be like. I was not in communication with anyone who attended college. The origins of my influence began with TV.

While attending college, I was influenced to study communication from a movie titled *Boomerang.* The film stars Eddie Murphy as Marcus Graham, a hotshot advertising executive. I was mesmerized by the attributes of his character: smart, funny, well-dressed, garnered extreme attention from women, and had an amazing job. I remember asking my college advisor for advice on getting into a career in advertising. She told me I would need to start with communication courses. Although these two examples may highlight a positive influence on action but, where there are pros, there are also cons.

Beauty (Media) and The Beast (Society)

The media has a manipulative way of defining beauty. It will not make a blatant statement or opinion on physical beauty. The manipulation of the message is disguised in the images we see.

- What does the hero look like in the movie?
- What does a love interest look like?
- What does their hair look like?
- What race is the character?
- What kind of car are they driving?
- How big is the house they live in?

When these images mirror or do not mirror who you are, the result can either create confidence or create insecurity.

Scarce or zero images in the media mirrored the gap between my teeth that I was born with. If it did exist, did the image reflect power, a love interest, a cool cop, or a superhero? I can recall people saying to me, *"Hey, how come you never got braces?"* or *"Why don't you get your teeth fixed?"* When I heard these questions, I would focus on the word "fixed." My answer would be, *"What told you I was broken or needed to be fixed?"*

The Influencer

As defined in today's society, an influencer is a person who can influence potential buyers of a product or service by promoting or recommending the item.

Corporations will pay top dollar to an influencer to promote their brand. The goal of influencer marketing is to create or feed into a desire, need, idea of acceptance, and status.

- ➢ You need this bottle of champagne to be cool like me.
- ➢ You need to wear this outfit to make a statement.
- ➢ You need to be at this party or on this trip.
- ➢ You need to have what I have to be considered successful.

When making this point to my classes, I would often use the Christian Louboutin shoe as an example. I would sarcastically ask, *"How are we living in a society where the color of the* bottom *of your shoe determines your status?"*

A student once replied in a combative tone, *"What is wrong with wanting nice things?"*

The answer was in the question itself. *"What told you it was nice, and why is it nice to you?"*

Understanding the manipulation of media is equivalent to knowing how a magic trick works. Once you are aware of how the trick works, you may become frustrated by how many people can be fooled by it.

Manipulation

On the topic of media and manipulation, specifically in regard to people of color, the Jim Crow laws and the creation of minstrel (Blackface character) performances must be considered in the manipulation process and the beginning of negative stereotypes regarding black people. Although I will not be able to dissect that theory as much as I would like in this book, I do feel it is important to mention it.

The History of Watermelon and Black People in America in Regards to Media

You may or may not have heard of how watermelons have become a racist trope. A "trope" refers to *any saying or image that gets used often enough to be recognized.*

Before it was sabotaged in the Jim Crow era, watermelon symbolized Black self-sufficiency.

As I have done in the past myself, you may ask, what does watermelon have to do with race? The stereotype that African Americans are excessively fond of watermelon was created for a specific purpose.

This stereotype was first created when enslaved people won their emancipation during the Civil War. Free Black people grew, ate, and sold watermelons. Many of them reaped great financial benefits from the sale of watermelons and, in doing so, made the watermelon a symbol of their freedom.

Racist white people, threatened by the idea of Black freedom, responded by making watermelon a symbol of Black people's perceived uncleanliness, laziness, childishness, and unwanted public presence. This racist trope then exploded in American popular culture through media in the form of derogatory print images, minstrel skits, and music performances that depicted Black people savagely eating watermelon.

Media and The Misrepresentation of Black Men

There is a clear connection to the way media (music, film, the news, books, etc.) represents Black men and boys to real-world outcomes.

- ➢ Media of all types can offer a distorted representation of the lives and reality of Black males. (How we are represented in the news and how we represent ourselves in entertainment and music can be distorted.)
- ➢ Media intake negatively affects society's understanding and attitudes related to Black males, sometimes including how Black males can even

understand who they are or who they are supposed to be.

➢ These distorted understandings and attitudes towards Black males lead to real-life consequences for them.

Interview With Angela Yee

I recall having the opportunity to interview a great friend and client of mine, Angela Yee. Angela Yee is a media journalist, entrepreneur, and one of the smartest people I have ever met in my life.

Below are a series of five questions I asked Angela regarding media and communication:

1. How do you define the word "Media?"

Traditionally, media should be trusted sources that provide unbiased information regarding current events and well-researched topics of interest. Media has morphed into influencers with a following communicating with their audience about things they may or may not be well-versed in. Personally, I hold the word media to a higher journalistic standard, but it has become an umbrella term.

2. If media is a vehicle for propaganda, is there a moral guideline for journalists?

The moral guidelines for journalists have gone out the window. I believe that if you want to find anything supporting your belief, no matter how ridiculous it may be, you can find that online somewhere. Journalists have been twisting truths to fit their narrative of what they choose to convey to their audience, to the point of blatantly lying. Of course, there are some journalists who are outstanding and do the work, but the amount of misinformation and trivial events that have been covered in politics, especially, has been disheartening.

3. **How does media influence the way people feel about themselves?**

Media supports popular beauty standards and can make you feel like you're not doing enough based on the metrics of success we see on TV and in marketing campaigns. With weight loss drugs, surgery, botox and fillers, celebs and personalities dripping in designer, we could end up chasing a dream and going broke while pursuing "happiness."

4. **How does the media gauge success?**

Media looks at your net worth and what you are doing *right now.* Is your current book a best seller, your movie a smash hit? Do you own a home, a Birkin?

5. **Why is media training significant to the success of any public figure?**

There will always be difficult questions to address or avoid and a need to express yourself effectively. An interview or public appearance can make people understand and like you more or turn others off completely. Media training can help you get right to the point, keep it interesting, and also show your true personality and what makes you relatable. And there is a level of comfort that comes with being prepared and confident, which media training can provide.

Hip-hop—Is It the Hero or the Villain?

What we consider to be entertainment might be education or miseducation to others. As a child of hip-hop culture and creator, it is highly important, and I'm obligated to state that I have received both an education and miseducation on who I am supposed to be as a Black man. I can credit hip-hop for assisting me on a path to self-actualization and the man I am today.

I must also show accountability and state that hip-hop also assisted me in potential self-destructive behavior. Hip-hop's positive or negative influence can circulate like the blood in our veins, reaching every organ in our body. Hip-hop flows through every channel and outlet of mass media, traveling through every country, state, and inner city, landing in the minds of the youth.

In my era of hip-hop music, we would celebrate the person coming home from prison more than the person going away to college. We idolize drug selling. We would take the name of Gangstas and make it a stage name. We have albums titled *"College Dropout,"* and songs called *"10 Crack Commandments."* We make records glorifying drug use. We do these things and accuse others of stereotypical behavior, but we must show accountability for what stereotypes we have created.

I loved A Tribe Called Quest. In 8th grade, Phife Dawg was my favorite MC, and then how our environment changed due to infection. Infection of street life, drugs, lust, power, false lifestyle, etc. All of this changed our environment, which changed the music. As I heard in a TED talk about a similar topic, *"Some of the music of this time was a result of a disenfranchised community who woke up on the wrong side of drugs, but we accepted these roles and glorified them."*

Jay-Z is quoted in his song, *Blue Magic, "Blame Reagan for making me into a monster."* Jay-Z is using this lyric to explain that the drug trade in America during the time Ronald Reagan was President caused him to become a drug dealer. Although there is some validity to this lyric, it is equally important to mention that we glorified this "monster." We put that monster inside a fancy car and gave it fancy clothes and jewelry. We made this "monster" cool.

There was a time in hip-hop culture when we would frown upon drug use. In this current era of hip-hop, drug use is highlighted and used as a measurement of how interesting an artist is. I can recall a young popular artist being asked during an interview about why the element of drug use was used inside his songs. His response to the question was shocking but thought-provoking. He stated, *"All the glorification of drug selling in the era of music prior to mine resulted in all the drug use in my era today. Who do you think those drugs were being sold to? Our parents."*

"Hip-hop is one of our generation's perpetrators, but it is also the art form that can turn this perception around."

~ Lecrae

4/23/24

In 2024, a hip-hop feud broke out between Kendrick Lamar, J Cole, and Drake. Kendrick drew first blood by taking aim at J Cole and Drake. J Cole released a response, and then after a week, he had a change of heart. J Cole decided to apologize to fellow hip-hop artist Kendrick Lamar for his role in creating a diss record. Cole expressed that engaging in such antics did not sit right with his spirit. The hip-hop community responded by ridiculing J Cole, saying that his apology did not align with the essence of hip-hop.

My personal thoughts were that Cole, who has reached the highest level of understanding himself, had a misstep on his path to self-actualization when he first created the record. I believe that disturbed him eternally. Once he was able to block out the noise surrounding the moment, he had a clear epiphany on what could come from such banter and did not want to engage further. I applauded Cole for having the highest form of self-awareness and not caring what others would think of his apology.

Are we the heroes, or are we the villains? Are we okay with all the messages we send in the content of the music? Do we say J Cole's apology isn't hip-hop?

5/4/24

Ironically enough, as the banter between Kendrick and Drake continued, the content within the music began to escalate in a venomous way. What should be considered off-limits in a musical dispute turned into an all-out war with women and children used as pawns. As this behavior continued, some spectators started to retract their statements about Cole, calling him a *prophet.*

My Thoughts

Hip-hop showed me

How to compete

How to dress

Hip-hop gave me power

Hip-hop told me what to eat

Hip-hop gave me liquor

Hip-hop gave me game

Hip-hop showed me how to sell crack

Hip-hop dropped out of college

Hip-hop gave me a gun

Hip-hop called me nigga

Hip-hop called my sister a bitch

Hip-hop gave me a Black President

Hip-hop made me rich

Hip-hop took me around the world

Hip-hop kept me on the block

Hip-hop sent my brother to jail

Hip-hop kept me out

Hip-hop must be able to self-evaluate

Hip-hop must be able to grow / Hip-hop is 50

Hip-hop has done all of this and more

So, it's ok if hip-hop can show remorse

In the role of the hero, it is obvious the amazing opportunities provided by hip-hop, but we must protect the education in the culture for the greater good. Hip-hop culture has created a pathway out of the neighborhoods that were designed to keep us trapped. It created a safe space where we are not discriminated against because of what we look like. We were celebrated because of what we looked like. Hip-hop culture is our very own country in which our music, fashion, food, our art, our expression, our authentic selves are the natural resources that so many are eager to benefit from.

For many of us, hip-hop culture created avenues of wealth in a country where we were brought to be slaves. It is the number one driving economic source in the world. Without hip-hop culture's influence, many corporations would not have the same success. The NBA and The NFL are examples of corporations that are widely successful not only because of the talent of the athletes alone but also because of the influence of hip-hop culture. The integration of hip-hop into these sports entities has had a clear impact on its success. From the music that is played in arenas, to the attendance and presence at games, to money that is generated every year at an NBA All-Star Weekend and Super Bowl Weekend, can apply a great percentage of credit to hip-hop culture. There isn't a fabric in this country that hip-hop influence isn't woven into. The culture is present in all industries, from technology to education, entertainment, and politics.

As Steve Stoute, owner of the ad agency Translation, mentioned in his book, *The Tanning of America, "hip-hop and its influence are responsible for electing The United States' first African American President, Barack Obama."*

Fat Joe, Derek Jeter, Ja Rule, Mongo, and Harold Wilkerson

"Chase Republic and Charlene Thomas of Def Jam Records light the Empire State Building Gold to Honor 50 years of Hip Hop"

Jadakiss, Ashanti, Ja Rule, and Harold Wilkerson

Source: @calligrafist

A press release reports that the trio was joined by Chase Republic founder Harold Wilkerson in partnership with Def Jam Records' VP of Marketin Dr. Charlene Thomas for the affair and the artists flipped the switch to light the historic landmark gold.

Applying the Theory of Hip-hop and Its Influence

MLB and Chase Republic

In May 2022, I was hired by Major League Baseball and the MLB store to curate and market an event that would take place inside the MLB flagship store on 5th Ave in Manhattan, New York. The event was to celebrate New Era's Baseball Caps on what they would call 59/FIFTY day.

Harold Koch, son of New Era founder Ehrhardt Koch, created the 59/FIFTY to make hats more uniform within MLB. Sources vary on the meaning of its name: it might be the cap's original catalog number, 5950. My role in this activation was to elevate awareness, increase traffic, and provide credibility within hip-hop culture and the MLB store via the fitted cap.

This is how the vision was executed.

"MLB 59/50 Day Presents: THE BLOCK PARTY"

The New Era baseball cap has always been a staple in the apparel of hip-hop culture, so on May 9th, we celebrated 59/FIFTY day with a block party/takeover of the MLB plaza and store along with an MLB Instagram live takeover. I hired hip-hop artists Jadakiss and Fabolous as two special guests to assist with the execution of my advertising vision. These two artists were widely recognized within the culture for wearing fitted caps in every music video and photo. This made the brand connection authentic. Jadakiss and Fabolous would advertise on their social media platforms confirming their attendance at the MLB store on this day. I asked them to wear their favorite team's fitted hat. Needless to say, both artists arrived wearing New York Yankee fitted hats and apparel. Because of the social media advertising, we would have over 500 customers arrive at the MLB store (which is triple the amount of customers they would normally have on a weekday) just to meet Jada and Fab and have them sign a NEW ERA hat. Myself, Jada, and Fab conducted a five-minute interview inside the store, which would air live on MLB's social media accounts. The host, an MLB exec, would ask how the baseball cap played a role in hip-hop fashion.

"Hip-hop culture will always hold the title in converting quantitative reasoning into qualitative thinking. (There's no data on cool)."

~ Harold Wilkerson

"From RUN DMC rocking no laces to tracksuits, we can turn gym wear into the runway."

~ Jadakiss

Jadakiss.

The fitted cap is another example of this.

"The fitted cap is hip-hop's crown."

~ Fabolous

Jadakiss, Harold Wilkerson, and Fabolous

Puffy Combs and the Shooting in New York

It was December 27, 1999, and I can recall the tragic shooting inside a club in New York as if it just happened. I remember receiving a call from my friend/manager, Nigel, telling me to get dressed and that he was coming to pick me up so we could go to the club with Diddy. When he arrived at my Bronx apartment, he told me we had to pick up Shyne on our way downtown. We picked up Shyne from Diddy's apartment on Park Avenue and headed to Diddy's studio to meet the rest of the partygoers.

We were having an amazing time inside the club. Diddy and his then-girlfriend, Jennifer Lopez, were engaging with the crowd, dancing and handing out glasses of champagne. I recall one part of the evening when I went over to Shyne and said, *"It's a lot of women in here tonight; who do you have your eye on?"* He said, *"No one. I have to be on point."* I was not sure why he responded that way, but in recollection, he seemed to be in that zone since Nigel and I had picked him up. The night progressed, and the chain of events took place. I remember leaving the club and seeing Shyne being cuffed by the police.

Please do not confuse this story with opening any wounds or paint a picture of Shyne, with whom I had a fair association. I tell this story because there are so many related stories in our culture. Does our media consumption negatively affect how Black males understand themselves and how these distorted understandings and attitudes towards Black males lead to negative real-world consequences for them? Did our hip-hop culture champion moments like this?

The Fyre Festival

The idea of the Fyre Festival was created to help promote the Fyre app. As I stated in Chapter 1, Intrapersonal Intelligence, although my job description and involvement was with Fyre Media, the platform, and not the Fyre Festival, I can recall meetings where the ingenious marketing would be discussed.

The plan was influencer marketing at its finest. Fyre Media hired some of the most influential socialites, including Kendall Jenner, Bella Hadid, and Hailey Baldwin. The idea was for these hand-picked celebrities to post a plain fire orange box on their Instagram page on a specific day and at a specific time. The caption would read, *"Fyre Festival,"* with a link to a website to purchase tickets. When the time came for all influencers to post their Fyre orange box to their millions of followers, a sea of orange flooded the timelines of Instagram. With consumer curiosity and the desire to be a part of something exclusive, along with all of the other emotions the media creates, millennials took action and clicked purchase!

The Fyre Festival will forever be infamously known, but the ingenious marketing strategy will possibly be duplicated by companies forever!

Chapter 5: Emotional Intelligence

"It takes more than intelligence to act intelligently."

~ Fyodor Dostoyevsky

Emotional intelligence is defined *as the ability to understand and manage your own emotions and those of the people around you. People with a high degree of emotional intelligence know what they're feeling, what their emotions mean, and how these emotions can affect other people.*

What Does It Mean to Be Emotionally Intelligent?

People who are emotionally intelligent are extremely aware of their own emotional states, even if those feelings are of negativity, frustration, or sadness. They are able to identify those feelings and manage them. They are aware of how their emotions can affect others.

Emotionally intelligent people are capable of not exposing others to those unpleasant emotions they are feeling. It's easier for a person in a negative state of mind to pull down the positive person. It's a much heavier lift for a positive person to pull up the negative person.

So, if you are the positive/joyful at heart person looking to lift up the negative person, the negative person will need to meet you halfway so the lift isn't all on you. They have to help themselves, want to be lifted, heal, and be better, and then the lift becomes lighter for the helper.

If they aren't seeking help, they will eventually pull you down to them.

Having a high degree of emotional intelligence means understanding that when someone is at war with themselves, and you are standing too close to them, you can become a casualty in that war.

Equally important, emotionally intelligent people are aware of the emotions that others may experience. Possessing a high frequency of emotional signals both from within and from one's social environment could make one a better friend, parent, leader, or romantic partner.

In today's society, there is a negative stereotype or stigma relating to the term or the idea of someone who is "emotional." Unfortunately, some will label being "emotional" as an unattractive attribute or character flaw. To label someone "emotional" without applying a sense of empathy or comprehension is, in fact, displaying a low sense of emotional intelligence. When emotional intelligence is absent from intrapersonal communication (the conversation within), the opportunity for an interpersonal connection will be challenging.

There should be less concern for the "emotional" person but more for the "emotionless."

The power is in self-emotional management, which results in managing the emotions of those around you. Emotions are involved in everything people do: every action, decision, and judgment. Emotionally intelligent people recognize this and use their thinking to manage their emotions rather than being managed by them.

Emotional intelligence has become a very important indicator of a person's knowledge, skills, and abilities in their professional and personal life. It is essential to their motivation, decision-making, successful management, and leadership. Thus, applying emotional intelligence will be essential on your path to self-actualization.

Emotional intelligence is an important ingredient in the recipe of your intrapersonal and interpersonal diet. As we understand, your intrapersonal communication is the relationship and conversion you have within yourself. Your interpersonal communication and relationships occur with others. Emotional intelligence must be present in both intrapersonal and interpersonal communication.

Interpersonal communication can be symbolized as a game of tennis with senders and receivers at each end of the net. The tennis ball serves as the message that the sender intends to relay to the receiver. When the tennis ball is in the sender's possession, they can manage the temperature of the exchange. As we stated in an earlier chapter, communication is irreversible. Once you hit the tennis ball over, once you send your message, that message no longer belongs to you. It now belongs to the receiver, and it now is for the receiver to interpret the meaning of your message.

A high sense of emotional intelligence means being able to understand the emotion you are feeling during any interaction. Being able to manage your emotions will, in turn, allow you to manage the emotions of the person you are engaging with. Once you identify that emotion, you can process it and then respond.

Applying the Theory

Maybe this true-life event will clarify the theory of emotional intelligence and the game of tennis.

The 94th Academy Awards ceremony took place on 7 March 2022. This particular ceremony was produced by Will Packer and Shayla Cowen, an associate of mine. This was a great accomplishment for them both, but unfortunately, it will be overshadowed by what is known as the slap heard around the world.

The slap I am referring to is the physical altercation between Will Smith and comedian Chris Rock.

I will attempt to relate this story to emotional intelligence.

Chris Rock opened up the Academy Award show with a small segment to warm up the crowd. During his segment, he cracked a joke about Jada Pinkett, who was seated with her husband, Will Smith. The joke made fun of her low, close-to-bald hairstyle. When Chris made the joke, the cameras panned to Jada and Will. It appeared that Will cracked a chuckle at the joke, but simultaneously, Jada looked disgusted. Will then stood up from his seat and walked towards the stage where Chris stood bewildered and slapped him in the face. Will turned back around and proceeded back to his seat.

Chris Rock stood shocked and said, *"Wow, Will Smith just slapped the shit out of me."*

Will then yelled from his seat, *"Keep my wife's name out of your mouth."*

Chris responded, *"It was just a GI Jane joke."*

Will repeated, *"Keep my wife's name out of your fucking mouth."*

This is the tennis exchange:

- Chris Rock serves the ball by telling the joke.
- Will receives the message (the tennis ball).
- Will then reacts in an impulsive way on national TV, gets up from his seat, and strikes Chris Rock (serves the ball back to Chris in the form of a strike).

- Chris Rock then serves the ball back to Will in a calm tone by saying, *"It was just a joke."*
- Will receives the message and serves the ball back in a more aggressive tone: *"Keep my wife's name out of your mouth."*

In this exchange, who would you say displayed a higher sense of emotional intelligence? What if when Will slapped Chris and turned his back, Chris hit him with the microphone stand?

What if, after Will yelled from his seat, Chris responded with a more harmful and harsh joke about the couple?

The Flow of Communication Relating to Emotional Intelligence:

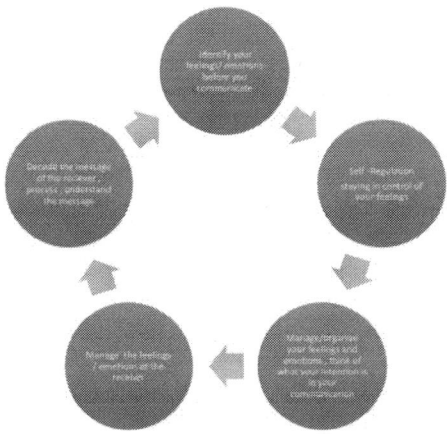

Some Key Factors That Will Assist With Emotional Intelligence:

- Be truthful with yourself about what you are feeling.
- Practice humility.
- Know your values.
- Hold yourself accountable.
- Listen with empathy.
- Have consideration.
- Separate the problem from the person.
- Identify when someone is disputing you instead of the problem.
- Understand what is best for you.

6 Tips for Dealing With A Difficult Person

1. Remain Calm

Benefit: Maintain self-control, avoid escalation of the problem.

How: The main goal in the face of a difficult person is to maintain your composure. The less reactive you are, the more you can use your better judgment. Take a few deep breaths, count to 10, or step away for a moment to collect your thoughts.

2. Separate the Person from the Problem

Benefit: Establish yourself as a person committed to solving problems with excellent people skills. Win more rapport, cooperation, and respect.

How: In every argument/discussion, there are two elements present: the relationship you have with the person and the problem or issue you are discussing. An efficient communicator knows how to separate the person from the issue. They can be soft on the person and firm on the issue.

Have you ever experienced arguing with a person who disagrees with every statement you make? They will argue with you if the sky is blue or not. This is when you can notice a person is in conflict with you and not the issue. When you're faced with this person, you must realize that there are stronger issues between you two. This awareness will help you to navigate the conversation more effectively, focus on finding solutions, and avoid getting drawn into unnecessary conflicts.

3. Use Active Listening

Benefit: Understand the other person's perspective, diffuse tension, and build rapport.

How: Pay attention to what the other person is saying, both verbally and non-verbally. Repeat what you've heard to ensure understanding, and ask clarifying questions to gather more information. This helps to prevent miscommunication and shows that you value the other person's perspective.

4. Avoid Taking It Personally

Benefit: Maintain objectivity, reduce emotional reactivity, and focus on finding solutions.

How: Remember that the other person's behavior or words are often a reflection of their own emotions, needs, or concerns. Try not to take their behavior personally, and instead, focus on finding solutions to the problem at hand.

5. Use "I" Statements

Benefit: Express your feelings and needs without blaming or attacking the other person.

How: Instead of saying *"you always"* or *"you never,"* try using *"I"* statements to express your feelings and needs. For example, *"I feel frustrated when..."* or *"I need..."* This helps to avoid blame and defensiveness and promotes a more constructive conversation.

6. Seek Common Ground

Benefit: Find areas of agreement, build rapport, and create a collaborative atmosphere.

How: Look for areas of commonality or shared interests with the other person. This can help to build rapport and create a more positive atmosphere for discussion. Try to find ways to compromise or find mutually beneficial solutions.

Chapter 6:
Leadership and Communication

Are leaders born, or are they made? What attributes make for a good leader? How do we define leadership?

It is important to differentiate between *leadership* and *power*. Some people often confuse the two, and at times, they can intertwine.

Positions of power may possess authority. To hold authority does not mean you also have guidance, direction, care, or encouragement. A police officer may hold a sense of power/authority. This does not necessarily mean the officer is a leader.

Leadership is the wise use of power. Leadership can exist without power, but there is no true power without the presence of leadership. True leadership is measured by influence. Your ability to influence will determine your level of leadership. The person who has the most influence is the leader of a group, not the boss, the CEO, the coach, the parent, etc. Those are just titles.

Your title will only buy you time among your followers (employees, friends, soldiers, etc.) When someone holds the title of boss or CEO, that just comes with respect. That respect and title will buy you time to prove if who you are is worthy of loyalty and leadership. Your decision-making, level of integrity, and emotional intelligence will play a major factor in someone's loyalty to you.

If you hold a title that you feel warrants leadership and loyalty, but you realize you are not the one that holds influence, you either befriend the person with the influence or try to get rid of them. By befriending the person who has the influence will allow you to carry out your agenda through them. If this strategy is not possible, you must look to remove them.

A fictional example of this is seen in the 2000 Dreamworks film *Gladiator,* starring Russell Crowe and Joaquin Phoenix. Maximus, played by Russel Crow, is a fearless and beloved army general of Julius Caesar. Commodus, played by Joaquin Phoenix, is the son of Julius Caesar and believes he is in line to be the next emperor once his father passes away. Maximus, the Roman general of the army, has influential leadership, which separates him from Commodus.

When Commodus' father feels his life is coming to an end as he grows older, he sends for his son, Commodus. Commodus thinks his father has sent for him to grant him the throne and to name him the next Caesar. To Commodus' heartbreaking surprise, his father tells him he will not name him Caesar. His father chooses Maximus to be the next leader of Rome. Caesar believes Maximus to be noble, wise, a moral man of integrity, and everything Commodus is not.

In a rage from his father's decision to choose Maximus over him, Commodus kills his father instantly by suffocation. He then declares himself as the new emperor and immediately sends for Maximus to have him swear his loyalty to him.

Unbeknownst to Commodus, before Caesar shares his decision with his son, he makes Maximus aware of the decision to name him as his successor instead. Once Commodus realizes that he cannot obtain Maximus's loyalty and that Maximus is the holder of all influence, he tries to kill him. He realizes that Maximus is the true leader, while Emperor Commodus may hold the title. Soon enough, all of Rome sees that Commodus is not worthy of leadership, and he dies at the hands of the true leader and emperor of Rome, Maximus, in a one-on-one battle inside the Colosseum.

"He studied to be a leader because he was a warrior at one time. Leaders can come up from the ranks. They have more empathy for those that follow them. The leader has been there before."

– Harold Wilkerson

Leadership in communication is the skill of modifying the attitudes and behaviors of others to meet shared group goals and needs.

a. To identify leaders, we need to determine who is influencing whom.

b. An effort to influence others is *attempted leadership*—only when others actually change does leadership become successful.

Leadership in group achievement helps clarify the difference between *leadership* and *persuasion*.

Persuasion involves changing attitudes and behavior through rational and emotional arguments. Since persuasive tactics can be used solely for personal gain, it is not always a leadership activity.

Different Styles of Leadership

An Authoritarian Leader...

- Maintains strict control over followers by directly regulating policy, procedures, and behavior.
- Creates distance between themselves and their followers as a means of emphasizing role distinctions.
- Believes that followers would not function effectively without direct supervision.

Examples

A police officer directing traffic, a supervisor instructing a subordinate to clean a workstation, etc.

A Democratic Leader...

- Engages in supportive communication that facilitates interaction between leaders and followers.

- Encourages follower involvement and participation in the determination of goals and procedures.
- Assumes that followers are capable of making informed decisions.
- Does not feel intimidated by suggestions provided by followers but believes that the contributions of others improve the overall quality of decision-making.
- Believes that two heads are better than one.

Examples

A group leader soliciting ideas from group members, a teacher using students' suggestions on a due date for an assignment, etc.

A Laissez-faire Leader…

Laissez-faire is a French word that roughly translates to *"leave them alone/let it be."*

- Offers little guidance, usually withdrawn.
- Sometimes results in poor productivity, cohesiveness, and satisfaction.
- A supervisor near retirement may become this type of leader.
- Some positives: Affords a high degree of autonomy and self-rule; at the same time, offers guidance and support when requested.

A Transformational Leader...

- Works with subordinates to identify needed change.
- Creates a vision to guide the change through inspiration.
- Executes the change in tandem with committed members of a group.

Chapter 7:
Power and Communication

VISION IS THE PRODUCT OF LEADERSHIP, AND POWER IS THEIR CURRENCY.

Power is not the same as leadership. Having power does not mean you have leadership. Power and leadership are obviously interdependent. However, they are not interchangeable. Power (the authority form of power) can exist without leadership.

A person of authority, such as a police officer, may possess a particular form of authoritative power. Similarly, a coach on a sports team may have the power to place a player on the bench. In both of these examples, that form of power does not mean either of the two is a leader.

"Leadership is the wise use of power. Power is the capacity to translate intention into reality and sustain it."

– Warren Bennis

Coercive Power

Coercive power is based on the ability to administer punishment or to give negative reinforcement. Examples of this power range from reducing status, salary, and benefits to requiring others to do something they don't like.

Coercion is most effective when those subject to this form of power are aware of expectations and are warned in advance about the penalties for failure to comply. Leaders using coercive power must consistently carry out threatened punishments.

The reward of power rests on the ability to deliver something of value to others. A reward must be desirable and attractive to serve as a sufficient motivator.

Legitimate Power

Legitimate power resides in the position rather than in the person. Persons with legitimate power have the right to prescribe our behavior with specified parameters. Examples of those with this kind of power include judges, police officers, teachers, and parents.

The amount of legitimate power someone has depends on the importance of the position they occupy and the willingness to grant authority to the person in that position. For example, an assistant may comply with a work request from their boss, but anything outside of that may come with resistance.

Expert Power

Expert power is based on the person, not the position, in contrast to legitimate power. Experts are influential because they supply needed information and skills. Those with credentials are more powerful than those without.

Referent Power

Referent power is role model power. When people admire someone, they confer upon the admired person the ability to influence their behavior. Referent power depends on feelings of affection, esteem, and respect for the individual.

Language Power

You can display your power or lack of power in your conversation. As Dr. Lillian Glass wrote in her book **Talking to Win,** *"The image you protect in your speech can determine whether a person will become your friend, lover, business associate, employer, or employee."*

Powerful Speech

Powerful speech makes speakers seem dominant and confident. Powerless speech is tentative (not certain) and submissive. It can be easily influenced or swayed.

Effective communication is not just about conveying information but also about maintaining power and control in a conversation. Powerful speech is about being calculated, concise, and intentional with our words, whereas powerless speech is about speaking excessively, revealing too much, and diminishing our authority. Avoid powerless speech in your rhetoric.

I'd rather ask for forgiveness than ask for permission.

This theory applies to business. When you are looking to execute a particular goal but are faced with thoughts of uncertainty, asking for permission from a client or partner may show signs of weakness. If a mistake is made while executing the goal, you should ask for forgiveness for the mistake rather than asking to even make the attempt.

Never say more than necessary.

The more you speak, the more of a chance you will expose thoughts not made for your listener's perception of you. The more you speak, the more common you will appear.

The principle *"never say more than necessary"* is a hallmark of power speech. This means:

- Being concise and direct.
- Avoiding unnecessary details or justifications.
- Maintaining control over the conversation.
- Preserving an air of mystery and intrigue.

By adopting the principle of *"never say more than necessary,"* we can project confidence, maintain control, and achieve our goals more effectively.

Never over-explain your actions.

Your actions should always be well-thought-out to avoid feelings of regret or remorse. Over-explaining your actions will make you appear to be unsure and weak.

Having hard conversations.

No one wants to be the bearer of bad news, but it is important to be able to have hard conversations. If you have disappointing news to share with a client or friend, do not wait to make the call. They may be upset, but in the end, they will respect you for not procrastinating in sharing the information.

Having difficult conversations is also a hallmark of power speech. It requires courage, empathy, and effective communication. In contrast, powerless speech often involves avoiding or delaying tough conversations, which can lead to more harm and damage in the long run.

The ability to have hard conversations is essential in both personal and professional relationships. When we procrastinate or avoid sharing disappointing news, we can:

- Damage trust and credibility.

- Create more problems and conflicts.

- Miss opportunities for growth and resolution.

On the other hand, having hard conversations demonstrates:

- A willingness to address challenges and find solutions.

I Apologize

The ability to show accountability when one is wrong is a hallmark of emotional intelligence, integrity, and character. When we apologize for our actions without making excuses, we demonstrate a strong sense of self-awareness. This courageous act empowers our intrapersonal intelligence.

Interestingly, a student once shared with me that she struggles to apologize because she believes it diminishes her power. However, I countered that knowing how to apologize is, in fact, a sign of strength, not weakness. By apologizing, we show that we value relationships, respect others' feelings, and are committed to personal growth.

In essence, apologizing is not about relinquishing power but about embracing our humanity, acknowledging our imperfections, and demonstrating our capacity for empathy, self-reflection, and resilience.

Kings should never discuss their issues with other kings in front of fools.

Discussing issues in front of fools will make the fool feel he has the right to an opinion on information that does not concern him.

Discussing one's issues or dealings with another person of prominence in front of those who lack your stature or attributes can be detrimental. When we share sensitive information with others, it can create a false sense of leading them to believe they have a right to an opinion or input.

In reality, not everyone is equipped to provide valuable insights or advice and should not have the privilege to be in your presence when certain conversations are taking place. By sharing our concerns or challenges with the wrong people, we expose ourselves to unsolicited advice or opinions.

In addition, we expose ourselves to:

- Unnecessary criticism or judgment.
- Misinformation or gossip.
- Hurting our authority or credibility.

Powerless Speech

Powerless speech involves:

- Rambling or excessive explanation.
- Seeking validation or approval.
- Revealing too much information.
- Losing control of the conversation.

Hesitations: *Uh, ah, well, um, you know.* These filler words clutter our speech and reduce our power.

Hedges: *Kind of, I think, I guess.* While useful when expressing uncertainty, hedges can dilute the impact of our message.

Example: *"I think we should have the report in by Friday."* (instead of *"Have that report by Friday."*)

Tag Questions: *Isn't, wouldn't it.* These indicate uncertainty and undermine our authority.

Disclaimers: *Don't get me wrong, I know this sounds crazy but.* While disclaimers can be useful in conversation, overusing them can signal a lack of confidence.

Apologizing unnecessarily: Starting sentences with *"I'm sorry"* or *"Excuse me"* when there's no need to apologize

Using passive voice: Constructing sentences in a way that avoids taking ownership or responsibility.

Example: *"Mistakes were made."* (instead of *"I made a mistake."*)

Making excessive use of polite language: Overusing words like *"please," "thank you,"* or *"could you"* to the point of sounding insincere.

Using vague language: Avoiding directness or clarity in our communication.

Example: *"I'll try to get it done soon."* (instead of *"I'll have it done by Friday."*)

Seeking constant validation: Asking for reassurance or approval excessively.

Example: *"Do you think this is a good idea? Do you really think so?"* (instead of *"I think this is a good idea."*)

Using minimizing language: Downplaying our achievements or contributions.

Example: *"It was no big deal."* (instead of *"I'm proud of what I accomplished."*)

Making excuses: Providing unnecessary explanations or justifications for our actions.

By recognizing and minimizing these forms of powerless speech, we can communicate more effectively, project confidence, and assert our authority.

Remember, power talk is not about being silent or unresponsive; it's about being intentional, strategic, and concise in our communication. By doing so, we can build trust, establish credibility, and maintain control in any conversation.

Chapter 8:
Persuasion and Communication

Persuasion is the strategic use of your communication to change or direct an individual's attitude or point of view to your own. It involves changing attitudes and behavior through logical, credible, or emotional arguments.

It is important to mention that *persuasion* and *manipulation* are not synonymous. When a person uses manipulation to direct an individual, they may only present their target with enough information that will leave them no choice but to see things their way. A manipulator will lie or withhold information to engineer their desired outcome.

When you are using persuasive communication, persuasion is ethically neutral. The strategy is not to lie, not withhold information, and to use the information you have and package that information in an attractive way using the elements/strategies of communication given ahead.

Three Elements/Strategies of Persuasive Communication

Logical Proof

In logical proof, arguments focus on facts and evidence. When you present facts in an argument, your listeners will likely resist counterarguments.

When using *logical proof* in persuasive communication, your success indeed relies heavily on your ability to use a clear and concise reasoning approach in your rhetoric.

Meeting your listener at their intelligence level and using examples they can easily understand and relate to is crucial in building a logical connection with them. This approach helps to:

- Establish credibility and trust
- Create a sense of clarity and understanding
- Build a logical and rational case for your argument
- Increase the persuasiveness of your message

Some effective techniques for using logiccal proof include:

- Using clear and concise language
- Providing concrete examples and illustrations
- Breaking down complex ideas into simple and manageable parts

- Using analogies and metaphors to explain complex concepts
- Providing evidence-based research and data to support your argument

Additionally, consider the following principles of logical reasoning:

- **The principle of causality:** Show how one thing leads to another
- **The principle of analogy:** Use comparisons to illustrate a point
- **The principle of precedent:** Use past experiences or examples to inform a decision
- **The principle of probability:** Use statistical evidence to support a claim

By incorporating these techniques and principles into your persuasive communication, you can build a strong logical case for your argument and increase your chances of success.

Emotional Proof

Emotional proof or motivational appeal appeals to your listener's feelings, needs, desires, and wants. It is a very powerful means of persuasion.

Emotional proof is a powerful tool in persuasive communication, and it relies heavily on your ability to connect with your audience on an emotional level. By using relatable rhetoric and a sentimental approach, you can tap into the emotional appeal of your listeners and create a deeper connection.

Great criminal lawyers are masters of this approach. They understand how to use emotional proof to create empathy and rapport with the jury, making it more likely for them to relate to their client's story and, ultimately, persuade them.

By using empathy and creating a space for the listener to put themselves in your shoes, you can:

- Build a deeper connection with your audience
- Increase emotional resonance and engagement
- Create a sense of shared understanding and experience
- Make your message more relatable and memorable

This approach requires a deep understanding of your audience's emotional needs, desires, and pain points. By acknowledging and validating their emotions, you can create a safe space for them to open up and be receptive to your message.

Some effective techniques for using emotional proof include:

- **Storytelling:** Share personal anecdotes or stories that illustrate your point and create an emotional connection.

- **Imagery:** Use vivid and descriptive language to paint a picture in the listener's mind.

- **Metaphor:** Use comparisons and analogies to create a deeper understanding and emotional resonance.

- **Emotional Appeals:** Appeal to the listener's emotions by using words and phrases that evoke feelings such as empathy, nostalgia, or excitement.

By incorporating these techniques into your persuasive communication, you can increase your chances of success and create a lasting impact on your audience.

Credibility Proof

Your credibility is the degree to which your audience regards you as believable. Your reputation is a powerful precursor to persuasive communication. When your reputation precedes you, it can either open doors or create obstacles. By establishing, creating, and protecting your reputation, you can significantly increase your chances of successful persuasion.

"Your reputation shows up in rooms before you do."

~ Harold Wilkerson

This means that people have already formed opinions and expectations about you before you even enter the conversation. By cultivating a strong, positive reputation, you can:

- Build trust and credibility with your audience
- Establish yourself as an expert or authority in your field
- Increase your influence and persuasive power
- Open doors to new opportunities and connections

Conversely, a damaged or negative reputation can:

- Create skepticism and mistrust
- Undermine your credibility and authority
- Decrease your influence and persuasive power
- Limit your opportunities and connections

By prioritizing reputation management, you can proactively shape public perception, build a strong personal brand, and increase your effectiveness in persuasive communication.

Goals of Persuasion

A. Persuasion refers to the process of influencing another person's attitudes, beliefs, values, and behaviors.

B. Strengthen or weaken attitudes, beliefs, or values.

C. To change attitudes, beliefs, or values.

D. To motivate action. Your goal is to get people to do something or to move them from one side to another.

Chapter 9:
Seductive Communication

To be continued...

Reviews on RateMyProfessor

"5.0. He was definitely one of my favorite professors ever. Amazing and very passionate about the class. He's very funny and chill. I would recommend him to anyone reading this."

"AMAZING LECTURES. HILARIOUS, CARING."

"Professor Wilkerson has clear lectures; he teaches what you have to know. I enjoyed his class; it was not stressful at all, and easy exams. I appreciate Professor Wilkerson and all his help during my semester. Thank you, professor."

"AMAZING LECTURES. GIVES GOOD FEEDBACK. CARING."

"He is the best! Makes you think critically about how to engage with others and yourself. If you need a communication course, take him."

"INSPIRATIONAL."

"Best class I've ever taken. I would recommend it to everyone! Assignments are incredibly fair. I can't say enough about this class. Just take it, and you won't regret it!!!"

"PARTICIPATION MATTERS. AMAZING LECTURES. HILARIOUS."

"Loved loved loved this professor; was very inspirational and funny. Had him as a night class, and was never tired or bored. Gave movies as homework assignments and made quizzes based on the movies and in-class discussions."

"AMAZING LECTURES. HILARIOUS. RESPECTED."

References

- https://www.inc.com/jayson-demers/7-subtle-conversation-habits-of-powerful-people.html

- https://www.verywellmind.com/what-is-self-concept-2795865

- https://tribemineblog.com/51-inspirational-networking-quotes/

- https://www.communicationstudies.com/communication-theories/social-penetration-theory

- https://education.nationalgeographic.org/resource/ecosystem

- https://www.theatlantic.com/national/archive/2014/12/how-watermelons-became-a-racist-trope/383529

- https://www.opportunityagenda.org/explore/resources-publications/media-representations-impact-black-men/media-portrayals

- https://marketbusinessnews.com/financial-glossary/media-definition-meaning/

- https://www.psychologytoday.com/us/basics/emotional-intelligence

Made in the USA
Monee, IL
01 May 2025

ff52ac62-baa2-4fef-b10a-ee3b4406fff5R01